# PRODUCT MARKETING MISUNDERSTOOD

# PRODUCT MARKETING
# MIS UNDER STOOD

*How to Establish Your Role,*
*Authority, and Strategic Value*

## RICHARD KING &
## BRYONY PEARCE

PRODUCT MARKETING MISUNDERSTOOD
*How to Establish Your Role, Authority, and Strategic Value*

ISBN   978-1-5445-2661-4   *Hardcover*
       978-1-5445-2660-7   *Paperback*
       978-1-5445-2659-1   *Ebook*
       978-1-5445-2679-9   *Audiobook*

# CONTENTS

# INTRODUCTION

Product marketing is not a new function. Just like sales, marketing, customer success, product, accounting, IT, and so on, it's been around for decades. The difference between product marketers and their cross-functional colleagues? Perception.

Ask anyone what sales reps do, and they'll tell you they sell stuff. Ask anyone what accountants do, and they'll tell you they're responsible for financial records. Ask anyone what product marketers do, and...you'll get wildly different answers at best, blank expressions at worst.

Anyone who understands product marketing understands the tremendous value it adds to organizations, but the problem is not enough people seem to *get* it, and that can make it notoriously hard for Product Marketing Managers (PMMs) to get the recognition they deserve.

Richard King built the Product Marketing Alliance to elevate the role of product marketing and address that very point. To double down on our mission, we (Rich King and Bryony Pearce, CMO) wrote this book to arm you with the tools you need to place yourself at the very core of your company so colleagues—past, present, and future—know, understand, and get exactly what you do.

Throughout this book, we've flipped common product marketing principles (positioning, messaging, research, personas, and so on) on their head to illustrate how product marketers plying our own trade can in turn help get ourselves real recognition.

By applying the advice outlined in the following pages, you will position yourself in such a way that rids you of the one-liners PMMs despise, like:

- "I know I asked a few times already, but what is it you do exactly?"
- "I have this slide deck I'm presenting tomorrow; can you please pretty it up?"
- "There's no time for customer research. Just launch it."

So, let's start at the beginning, define product marketing, and get everyone speaking the same language before we dive into the details.

# IT'S TIME TO DEFINE

To ensure alignment, it's key that you can define product marketing. You want to be able to set expectations company wide and by department. Then—and only then—will you be in a position to truly set yourself and your function up for success.

In this section of the book, we will:

- Look at key definitions.
- Craft your own definition.
- Share our "What is product marketing?" slide deck.

## WHAT IS PRODUCT MARKETING?

This is a question all product marketers get asked all the time... but in reality, there's no set answer. Every product marketer seems to have a different viewpoint and definition, and that's because product marketing can differ quite significantly from company to company. Factors such as growth stage, type of customers (i.e., B2B, B2C, B2D), type of product (i.e., physical, SaaS, both), industry, company culture, and more can all impact how a product marketer goes about their day-to-day.

Here's the PMA definition:

> *Product marketers are the driving force behind getting products to market—and keeping them there. Product marketers are the overarching voices of the customer, masterminds of messaging, enablers of sales, and accelerators of adoption. All at the same time.*

And here are a few more definitions from experts in the PMM profession:

> *Marvin Chow, Vice President, Global Marketing at Google*: "The ultimate role of a PMM is to liaise between the product engineers and the end user. PMMs should be an expert on the user and their needs. Great PMMs champion the voices of all users and celebrate and elevate diverse perspectives. During the go-to-market process, PMMs should own the launch plan, working to make the product a reality for all users."

> *Anand Akela, Product Marketing Leader at Nutanix*: "Product marketing is responsible for taking a product or solution

to market by building the go-to-market strategy and driving its execution via differentiated product messaging and launches, thought leadership and awareness, demand-gen support as SME, and sales enablement."

*Carol Carpenter, VP of Product Marketing at Google Cloud:* "The role and value of product marketing is to express the distinct value of our solutions to customers. Expression of value."

Next, we'll take a look at the individual areas of responsibility that ladder up to these outcomes.

## CORE RESPONSIBILITIES OF A PMM

Every year, more than two thousand product marketers take part in our State of Product Marketing report, which provides invaluable insights into what product marketers' main responsibilities are and enables us to give an incredibly accurate overview of the product marketing role as a whole.

On the back of these findings, product positioning and messaging were identified as the core elements of the product marketing role, with 92 percent of people taking part identifying this as one of their main responsibilities. Managing product launches (79 percent), creating sales collateral (78 percent), and customer and market research (72 percent) also scored highly.

| | 2021 | 2020 |
|---|---|---|
| **Product positioning and messaging** | 92% | 92.6% |
| **Managing product launches** | 79% | 85.1% |
| **Creating sales collateral** | 78% | 73.8% |
| **Customer and market research** | 72% | 70.9% |
| **Storytelling** | 60% | 59.8% |
| **Reporting on product marketing success** | 60% | 59.1% |
| **Content marketing** | 51% | 54.9% |
| **Customer marketing** | 40% | N/A |
| **Website management** | 33% | 34.9% |
| **Onboarding customers** | 20% | 27.7% |
| **Product roadmap planning** | 19% | 26.8% |
| **Other** | 6% | 8.4% |

As we touched on a little earlier though, the role varies from industry to industry, company to company, and product to product, so what's a priority for someone else might not necessarily be a priority for you.

For one product marketer, creating sales collateral might make up 60 percent of their job, and for another, it might account for just 25 percent of it. The stage your company is at will play a huge role in this too. If you're at a startup, for example, you'll probably get stuck with a bit of everything. But as companies start to expand and become more established, the role is more focused, and you might just be primarily tasked with overseeing a product's messaging, or go-to-market strategy, or research, for example. You'll also have a lot more subject-matter experts at your disposal at these big organizations, and that means you might not have to physically create the content marketing assets yourself. It might be done by a dedicated copywriter, for example, or you might have SEO teams who take care of your organic strategy, and so on. Who knows what those variances will look like down the line? But for now, you could say it's part and parcel with the function.

## THE PRODUCT MARKETING FRAMEWORK

When executed right, product marketing:

1. Represents the voice of the customer—before, during, *and* after launch.
2. Clearly articulates a product's value in a way that resonates with the market.
3. Drives product adoption and advocacy.

And of course, none of this happens by itself. To say the role of a product marketer is varied would be an understatement, to say the least. In a previous life, we're certain PMMs used to be professional jugglers.

PMA's Product Marketing Framework encapsulates all the moving parts of the product marketing role into one handy diagram. This framework defines the five fundamental phases of product marketing:

- Discover
- Strategize
- Define
- Get set
- Grow

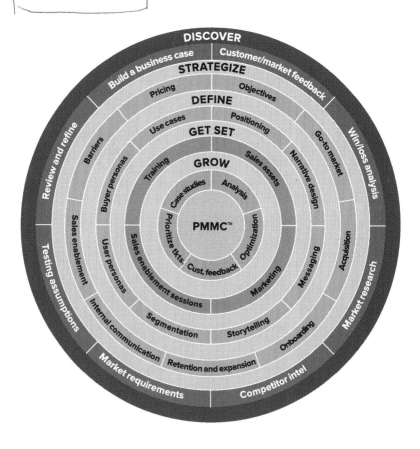

If you're new to product marketing, we really would recommend familiarizing yourself with the full framework to get a better understanding of the end-to-end picture. In the meantime, though, here's a whistle-stop tour of each layer:

- **Discover**: This is the stage in which you gather the info and insight to turn your assumptions into an educated hypothesis. Customer feedback and sussing out the competition are just two of the key elements involved—and they're both product marketing gold dust.

- **Strategize**: Whether it's product-market fit, your GTM plan, or your pricing, strong product marketing always comes with a strategy.

- **Define**: This is all about identifying your positioning, messaging, personas, etc. and applying what you garnered from your discovery stage to shape customer journeys and communications.

- **Get set**: Here, it's time to harness all your hard work thus far with training, sales enablement sessions, and marketing campaigns so your team is equipped to take the GTM by the horns and run with it.

- **Grow**: This is where your post-launch process needs to kick in, to ensure your product continues to flourish and evolve in its market.

Before we move on, one final, important thing to note is the *shape* of the framework. It's a circle for a reason: to express the fluidity of the product marketing role. The best-known products out there aren't a success by chance; they're the result of continuous iteration, and that's why a PMM's role is present *throughout* the product life cycle.

If you want to explore the framework in more depth, head to our hub using the QR code below or this link: *productmarketingalliance.com/ product-marketing-framework*.

## WHAT'S YOUR DEFINITION?

Now that we've explored our definition and that of other PMMs, take a few minutes to work on your elevator pitch definition— what is product marketing? Write it below—it can be succinct or all-encompassing. (As well as defining the role in your definition, try to sum up the value of a product marketer too.) This exercise will come in handy if you decide to do a company roadshow and create your own "What is product marketing?" deck— coming later in the book.

_____

_____

_____

_____

----

----

----

----

----

----

## BREAKING DOWN YOUR DEFINITION

Along with having a standard definition of product marketing, it can be beneficial to tweak this so that you have several slightly different definitions for the key cross-functional stakeholders within your company.

Think about the five core departments—sales, customer success, product management, marketing, and engineering. You will provide a tremendous amount of value to each of these departments, but that value will come in different forms. So, ask yourself, "How can I demonstrate the value I offer to each of them in a way that relates and resonates with their own unique needs and objectives?"

It's key that all departments understand what product marketing does, not just the C-suite. If people don't understand what you do, you'll be marginalized, and you won't be able to thrive—and neither will they.

Take some time to analyze your current relationships with key departments in your company, and jot down your definitions for each below. Remember, this definition doesn't have to resemble the value you currently add if you're not being given the autonomy to do so. These definitions should be of the value you could add if you were set up to do so. The idea is that having and sharing these segmented definitions will illustrate your impact and open the right doors.

My product marketing definition for sales:

_____

_____

_____

My product marketing definition for customer success:

_____

_____

_____

My product marketing definition for product management:

_____

_____

_____

My product marketing definition for marketing:

_____

_____

_____

My product marketing definition for engineering:

_____

_____

_____

Depending on the size and nature of your organization, you might also have a direct line of communication with your CEO. Needless to say, securing their backing will make your life _a lot_ easier.

Here's a great quote from Elizabeth Brigham, former Head of Product Marketing (Software) at Morningstar, on why product marketing is important. This is a great excerpt, and we use it a lot. If you're struggling to get your CEO to understand some of the fundamental problems PMMs solve, we suggest sharing this, or paraphrasing this, with them. If you're planning on doing the product marketing roadshows we mentioned earlier in the book, those sessions would also be a great time to voice this.

_There are quotations out there that say anywhere between 80–90 percent of new businesses fail, whether that's a_ *startup, new product line, or new business being launched within an existing company. Some of those reports went back and asked CEOs or others within the C-suite, well, why do you think you failed?*

*The number one answer that comes back is product-market fit, and the way I break that down is by saying, well, you've got a product and a lot of people might think this is the cool, new, shiny thing, and a lot of times what I've seen, especially in smaller, more nascent companies, is the founder or person who built it had that problem and then tries to go find a market. Whereas product marketing actually assesses the market, what sort of core competencies that organization already has, and then pulls that empathy and understanding of the market into what we should go and build. Product marketers fundamentally understand there's an acute pain point going on for which people are willing to pay for a solution, and that is truly the value that a product marketing manager brings to the table.*

*It's taking down the risk or lowering the risk of investing a lot of money, whether it's in people or product development or acquiring something new, and de-risking that investment.*

As a product marketer, you already knew this. But if those around you do not, use this, share it, and help them understand.

My product marketing definition for the CEO:

_____

_____

_____

## THE "WHAT IS PRODUCT MARKETING?" SLIDE DECK

Now that you have those definitions, it's time to do something with them—it's no good just understanding what your role is to those departments; they need to understand it too. To do this, many product marketers adopt a "roadshow" type approach, whereby they book time with those key teams, deliver a tailored presentation, and ensure everyone in the room is on the same page when it comes to product marketing's deliverables and value.

Here's a slide deck we created for the Product Marketing Alliance to give you a jumping off point. Of course, these kinds of decks will need to be hyperpersonalized to your orga-  nization setup. Just head to the QR code to get a digital version you can adapt. Or if you're reading this book digitally, head to *this link*.

### WHAT PMMS DO AND DON'T DO

As we mentioned earlier, the product marketing role does vary greatly from one company to the next, but it can be helpful to consider some DOs and DON'Ts.

Duong Tran, Marketing Manager at RBC Ventures, is a full-stack digital and product marketer, skilled in both high-level strategic planning and hands-on tactical execution. His DOs are:

- I need to become best friends with the product team.
- I should strive to be involved as early as possible.
- I must understand the market and talk to customers.
- I ought to own and surface the narrative of any new products/features.

And his DON'Ts are:

- I shouldn't consult with the ones building the products (Dev/Ops).
- I don't ever want to launch a product with no clear metrics/KPIs.
- Never ignore what happens after post-launch.
- Don't let go—I must drive the decisions.
- Never be confined to one specific task—PMMs should be fluid and wear multiple hats.

Take a few minutes to consider your own DOs and DON'T. Writing them down can help you remain focused and will helpfully perfect the art of saying no (a topic we'll discuss later in the book).

My DOs:

- _____
- _____
- _____
- _____

My DON'Ts:

- _____
- _____
- _____
- _____

Now that you've got your slide deck, you know what product marketers do and don't do, and you've got your definitions, nothing is stopping you from confidently delivering your own company tour.

Next, we'll go back in time a bit and explore the evolution of the product marketing role.

# CHAPTER 2

# THE PAST, THE PRESENT, AND THE FUTURE

There has *never* been a better time to be a product marketer. The product marketing role is on an aggressive upward trajectory, and many are now saying PMMs are primed to be the best chief marketing officers, chief strategy officers, and even chief executive officers. Not a bad career path, eh?

In this section of the book, we will:

- Delve into the history of product marketing.
- Look at predictions for the future.
- Demonstrate how important it is to show people your value as a product marketer.
- Highlight why internal positioning is so important.

## THE EVOLUTION OF PRODUCT MARKETING

It's always a good idea to start at the beginning, but when it comes to product marketing, no one is exactly sure where the beginning is. How it has evolved over the years and gotten to where it is today is up for debate.

That said, product marketing has actually been around for twenty or more years, with global giants like Apple, Canon, and Microsoft realizing the role's value earlier than most—although in its early days, it was commonly called technical marketing. In simple terms, the technical marketing of old was any method of marketing that focused on the key features and specifications of a product. The intention was to attract customers who already had a basic technical appreciation for the product.

Back then, these products were usually different types of enterprise hardware, such as servers. Product marketers had to know how to explain the benefits of buying a piece of hardware and having it physically located within the customer's organization. But that wasn't traditional marketing. Traditional marketing was email, TV, radio, print ads, and so on.

In short, product marketers had to have a technical understanding of the product and how to sell it—so the role's been around a long time; it was just called something different previously.

Yoni Solomon is a leading voice in the product marketing sphere. Formerly the Director of Product Marketing at G2, he's since made the move into the illustrious C-suite (which we're gradually starting to see more and more of, further demonstrating the prowess of the PMM function). Now the Chief Marketing Officer at Uptime.com, Yoni spoke to us about the evolution of product marketing. He said:

> As with everything in life, product marketing has had to evolve with the times and state of technology. It was a different world in the 1990s when go-to-market was being defined for software and technology companies.
>
> Back then, the average software release frequency was approximately three months. Today, the average release cycle is just three weeks. Platform updates can now happen in just minutes, or seconds. Even AI is now writing its own code.
>
> We've gotten better at building software—faster. And in doing so, product marketing had to evolve to keep up. In doing so, it's become a company's most-informed, fastest-moving, and most cross-functional team—which is needed if it's going to align product management, marketing, and sales teams to go-to-market with new capabilities.

Another key shift we're seeing is the perception of product marketing being seen as a primarily tactical role (old view) to an essential, strategic cog (new view).

We spoke to Jeffrey Vocell, Director of Product Marketing at Iterable, about his personal experiences with the progress that's been made over the last decade or so.

He said in some of his former product marketing roles, the companies would define product marketing in a way where he was primarily doing content generation—writing blog posts, case studies, or various content for that company.

Fast-forward to today, Jeffrey believes the role is really centered around strategy, and not any specific kinds of tactics. That said, being responsible for fundamentally bringing new products to the market, helping to sell those products, and helping explain the true narrative of the products inevitably entails a healthy blend of both strategy and tactics. The highlight for PMMs here is the increasingly prominent seat at the strategic table.

As you can see, it's clear product marketing is having a renaissance alongside the development of the SaaS landscape as well. Over the last seven years, SaaS has exploded, with most businesses speaking the same language or working from the same templates. Now, the only differentiator is the product marketer who is getting it right and enabling their company to stand out in an increasingly competitive crowd.

If we rewind to five years ago, a product marketer's main role was to bring a product to market. Today, customers want their voices heard, and they have more ways than ever before to do just that, thanks to the emergence of many online and off-line platforms. The most engaged customers take their voice one step further and seek to collaborate directly with the businesses they interact with. The most successful product marketers embrace this type of listening and collaborate fully and with enthusiasm—because any PMM worth their salt will tell you this is, hands down, the best route to achieve next-gen outcomes. While we're not suggesting assumptions should be eradicated, it's clear to see the voice of the customer is the cornerstone of long-term success.

Div Manickam, Portfolio Messaging (Product, Industry, and Solutions) and Platform Evangelist, believes product marketing has evolved even further into portfolio marketing. She states:

> Many of us product marketers pride ourselves on being well-rounded and being able to turn our hand at anything, as we regularly jump from one project to another—from messaging to analyst relations to customer interactions. As such, the specific roles and responsibilities of product marketers are constantly evolving.
>
> In the past, we were focused simply and solely on a product. During my time at my last company, this had progressed from just a particular product to also include solutions, industries, and services. Recently, I've even had conversations with product marketing leaders that have shifted to referring to the role as "portfolio marketing," which encompasses the industry in general.

*Just like we have specialized teams for demand generation that didn't exist a decade or so ago, it's time to find our strategic space in the product or marketing organization. Based on my recent experiences, our PMM team was integral to the messaging and positioning efforts not just within product or marketing, but also under the COO/Services org. This makes me wonder if we need to think bigger and even create a separate org for this team that is cross-functional and not limited by just the marketing, product, or services functions in a company.*

## THE BIGGEST FRUSTRATION

The universal pain point in product marketing is that people just don't understand the value of the role. A few years ago, some people may have considered product marketing an extension of a technical marketer, or someone who was good at shoving slide decks together. Sadly, some people may still have this view, and it's up to us to change that uninformed perspective.

Jim Walker, Vice President of Product Marketing at Cockroach Labs, believes there are seven main reasons why product marketing is often misunderstood:

1. Every organization is different.
2. Product management and product marketing overlap.
3. The emergence of content marketing.
4. Size/stage of company and marketing organization.
5. Historical expectations.

6. Every industry is different.
7. People and expertise.

He says that what's helped him explain product marketing to non-product marketers is using a broader definition: "Product marketing is the process of building and delivering a core narrative."

How a product marketer looks at their role can also be impacted by where the role of product marketing sits within the organization. A product marketer who works for the global headquarters of a company will have a very different experience than a PMM from a regional office.

The global headquarters is the epicenter of where decisions are made, and a product marketer based there would be close to the product team and have the most influence. They are more likely to be able to shape how the product is made to meet market fit, and they can bring customer feedback and other insights directly into the product.

A product marketer at a regional office doesn't always have the same feeling of empowerment as their colleagues at HQ and typically won't have the same level of influence. Their role will be focused on regional execution because they aren't where key decisions are being made.

If this is sounding familiar to you, don't despair. Many PMMs have been there, and here's how Harvey Lee, Product Marketing and Innovation Director at Avast, turned it around during his time at Microsoft:

*Although I was in a regional role at Microsoft, I was in an EMEA role (Europe, the Middle East, and Africa), and I felt there was misattribution or misunderstanding to the value I was bringing, not in the regional team to my direct managers, but in the US team where the headquarters were. They were so far away, and we didn't tour that often.*

*I decided to reposition myself specifically to address that issue. I did this by asking for presentation time at certain meetings during one of my frequent trips to Seattle, and they were more than happy to hear from regions because they didn't get enough feedback.*

*So here was me going "I want to share," and I would share what I did, how I do what I do, and what the results were and what I did over time. It didn't take that long—maybe half a dozen meetings at most—but I repositioned myself in their eyes as part of their team, not separate from their team.*

*I didn't want them to look at me as some regional outpost they don't understand because they don't know anything. I wanted them to look at me as part of their own team. I just happened to sit somewhere else and that was the trick. Once I turned that around, every conversation I ever had after that usually involved them phoning me instead of me chasing them. And*

*I became their trusted advisor, and that was really key that in their eyes I became their trusted advisor for the European market. Because they didn't see me as different from what they were.*

Another frustration for product marketers can be the lack of understanding and appreciation that goes into all the activities that happen before a launch. After a launch, it's easy for people in your org to get caught up in key metrics like MQLs, SQLs, deals won, website traffic, sales demos booked, etc. But the frustrating part can be that product marketing doesn't necessarily get the credit for any of these. MQLs, SQLs, and site traffic often get attributed to marketing. Deals won and sales demos to sales. In reality, product marketing is the linchpin to each of these. Without the right positioning, messaging, personas, sales content, and more, the above metrics aren't possible, but these pre-steps can be overlooked.

As Jeffrey Vocell, Director of Product Marketing at Iterable, likes to look at it, product marketers are the "quarterbacks" of a launch or new feature. Although you're not necessarily sending the email to customers or prospects, you're arming the relevant teams with what needs to go into those emails, what segmentation strategy should be used, and so on.

If you're feeling like your role is being glossed over when it comes to launches, consider setting up retrospective meetings, and in those retrospectives, be sure to emphasize why you think your positioning, messaging, persona, segmentation, pricing, and other strategies worked. Of course, it's a team effort, and we're not suggesting this is all about showboating your skills, but don't be afraid to claim credit where credit's due. If you don't, who will?

## PREDICTIONS FOR THE FUTURE

While we don't profess to have a crystal ball that predicts the future of product marketing, we do have our own hunches—and that of the thousands of PMMs in our community.

We're already seeing more and more product marketers move into the C-suite, one of the most prominent being Greg "Joz" Joswiak's appointment as Apple's Senior Vice President, Worldwide Marketing (previously Apple's Head of Product Marketing). We've also witnessed several PMMs within our community making the move, some into chief marketing officer roles, others into chief strategy officer roles. This isn't going to stop. We mentioned it earlier in the book, but product marketers really are primed to fill these kinds of strategic positions, and as more and more organizations realize this, more and more PMMs will enter the C-suite.

Cody Bernard, Senior Manager of Product Marketing at Drift, agrees: "Gone are the days of the traditional path to a CMO role (i.e., demand-gen). Product marketing is a core strategic function of high-performing marketing teams that helps put the business in the best position to win, and we will see product marketers rewarded for it."

And so does Jarod Greene, VP of Product Marketing at Highspot, who believes product marketing will see at least a five-times increase of presence with the C-Suite and a three-times increase of presence with the board of directors.

In a similar vein, we also believe the product marketing role itself could soon form part of the C-suite. Whether it be chief product marketing officer, chief portfolio officer, or other, it deserves its place. In line with this, companies will start expanding (or creating) product marketing functions within the company. We won't ladder up to product or marketing; product marketing will have its own place, and won't run the risk of potentially being hindered by one or the other. In addition to this, we predict product marketing leaders will start to expand their influence within their organizations by taking on new responsibilities and functions, such as customer marketing.

Our third prediction is less of a prediction, and more of a continuance. We're already seeing the perception of product marketing shifting into more of a strategic one. In the coming years, this will not just continue but accelerate. Members of the senior leadership team will understand the true value of product marketing isn't just following the strategies that come from above but shaping and building those strategies themselves.

Our fourth prediction is that companies will begin to recruit product marketers earlier—especially startups. All too often, PMMs are brought into the fold too late, and by then, the business has lost on differentiation and connecting with their market. Many believe PMMs should be the first marketing hire—the more people understand the importance of product marketing, the more this will happen.

For prediction number five, we'll pass the mic over to Lauren Culbertson, Co-Founder and CEO at LoopVOC:

> *Product marketing will evolve as more and more companies move towards product-led growth, the movement away from traditional sales cycles and towards relying on your product to acquire, activate, and retain customers. There are several trends that point towards the shift to product-led growth. According to a 2020 study by TrustRadius, the majority of B2B tech buyers are now millennials who are two times more likely than older generations to discover a product by searching online. The study also found that 87 percent of these buyers want to self-serve part or all of their buying journey without talking with a sales representative and consult an average of about seven information sources before making a purchase, relying most on product demos, vendor websites, and free trials.*

> *Even large enterprise buyers now expect to try and evaluate software in an easy, frictionless way. As a result,*

*product marketers will shift away from sales enablement and towards product enablement—ensuring buyers experience meaningful outcomes while using their products. They will become more responsible for active usage and ensuring the right leads become customers based on segmentation criteria. PMMs will be less incentivized on the quantity of content, sales tools, and launches they produce, and more incentivized on the quality of these tactics to drive active and engaged users.*

*They will increasingly use quantitative and qualitative data to understand customer needs and behaviors and use that intel to make GTM decisions that increase product stickiness and adoption. They will use this data to create more granular customer segments and targeted solutions based on a customer's needs and how they use the platform.*

*And most importantly, the movement towards PLG will give PMMs the opportunity to rise up from executing on sales activities and fire drills, and instead act as the architect of growth for their products.*

By this point in the book, you should have a firm understanding of what product marketing is and isn't, where it has come from, where it is now, and where it will be in the future. Now that we've laid the groundwork, for the final section of this chapter, we'll circle back to the essence of this entire book—why internal positioning matters—before moving on to the all-important *how*.

## WHY DOES INTERNAL POSITIONING MATTER?

It's so vital to own your internal positioning. If you don't do it for yourself, no one else will do it for you. In doing so, you'll get to influence and have your voice heard within your organization. You'll get to be fully involved and fully contributing. And you'll get to reach your professional potential.

Product marketers add the most value when they are:

- Immersed in the product development process.
- Putting strategic planning and creative problem-solving skills to work.
- Tapping into customer empathy and competitive insights through extensive research.
- Adapting to the constant flux around flexible delivery timelines or market dynamics.
- Nailing product positioning and messaging.
- Continually enhancing writing and presentation capabilities and skills.
- Outlining objectives and key results (OKRs) around go-to-market strategy, sales enablement, and product adoption.

However, none of this is possible if you're not positioned in the right way. If product management doesn't understand the value you bring to the product development process, they'll be less likely to proactively bring you into the loop. If senior stakeholders don't realize how valuable your insights are when it comes to broader strategies, you won't be given a voice. If the wider organization doesn't understand the true merit of your positioning and messaging work, neither will be adopted. You get our drift. Every single one of these points will hinder how much of a difference you can make in your company, and every single one of these points can be addressed with the correct positioning.

When C-suite members clearly value and define the role of product marketing and know what it is about, it isn't an accident. It is usually the result of the hard work and dedication of product marketers within their organization. They have positioned themselves in such a way that they achieve a greater level of understanding and respect from senior leaders.

If you wish for the same in your organization, follow this book and use all the guidance contained within it. By implementing the advice, tactics, and learnings outlined, you should be able to bring about a 360° change. When you have a C-suite that is bought in, you'll be able to do your job better. This in turn will not only make you look better but could also help you move up the career ladder at an accelerated pace.

# CHAPTER 3

# WINNING OR LOSING... YOUR CHOICE

If a PMM can nail their internal positioning, they are able to accomplish a lot, and the whole company benefits. But if they can't, and instead they just "exist," everyone misses out.

In this section of the book, we will:

- Explore what it means to be a sole PMM.
- Find out how best to build a PMM team and where they should sit.
- Share how to structure your team for success.
- Highlight the five key product marketing personas.

## POSITIONING YOURSELF WHEN
## YOU'RE THE SOLE PMM

One in five of the PMMs who took part in the PMA's State of Product Marketing Report said they are the sole product marketers in their companies, and there are many positives to being the first PMM in an early-stage company. You have a lot of creative freedom on how the internal structures will be set in place and are able to lead decisions on the GTM strategy and have direct communication with the main stakeholders of the company. However, while this can be great, the success of this is heavily reliant on you.

If you're a one-man PMM band, you will likely be faced with a couple of challenges. First, you will be solely responsible for positioning the product marketing function to the wider business. Hopefully, the function will grow over time, so accurately setting expectations and illustrating value when you're the first hire can be hugely important for perceptions down the line.

You may be joining a company full of colleagues who have never worked with product marketers before. You may be faced with some people who have never heard of the role, but others who have—but perhaps their experiences weren't reflective of the real PMM role. Or you could be greeted with an entire company truly clued up on the role, responsibilities, and value of PMMs.

Whichever landscape you're met with, it is paramount you dedicate sufficient time—from your first day—to address this. The quicker you get your organization up to speed on what it is you do, how you can benefit various stakeholders, and what you pledge to deliver, the quicker—and easier—you will be able to get to work on delivering results.

To act on this, we would recommend doing a roadshow. In your first few weeks, book in some time with key stakeholders and teams and:

- Get to know them—building personal relationships is key.
- Chat with them about their goals and challenges.
- Break down what it is you do and why it's important.
- Explain how what you do will help you, them, and the entire company reach their goals.

If you get this piece right, you're on the path to a prosperous relationship based on a mutually shared—and accurate—understanding of what you've been hired to do.

One thing you don't want to do in this first meeting is over-promise and under-deliver. To strike the right balance and not put your relationship on the line, we would suggest keeping things fairly top level at this stage. After you've heard their goals and challenges, talk about how product marketing slots into those areas, but don't promise X, Y, or Z on the spot. Let the individual know that you'll come back to them in a week or two with a detailed action plan of what you can do, how you will do it, how it will help them achieve their goals and remove their challenges, and a timeline of when you can execute on this plan. For you, this will ensure that you're confident with the strategy you're suggesting and confident that you'll deliver it. For your stakeholder, it fosters a sense of trust and gratitude that their input is being heard and inserted into broader plans, and this can only be a positive for your relationship and position with them in the future.

The second challenge you may encounter is workload. When you're the sole PMM, and you've got the wider org bought into what you do, you may find yourself with a very positive problem: everyone is so impressed with the value of your role that they want more and more from you. They come to you with requests, they want you in their meetings, and they want your input on their projects. All of this is great, but there is only so much one PMM can do—more on this in the next section.

You will also need to become more of a "specialist generalist." If you do not have any product marketing teammates, the suite of core PMM responsibilities will likely fall on your shoulders. As per our research with thousands of product marketers, these core areas are:

- Product positioning and messaging.
- Managing product launches.
- Creating sales collateral.
- Customer and market research.
- Storytelling.
- Reporting on key metrics.

- Content marketing.
- Website management.
- Onboarding customers.
- Product roadmap planning.

Suffice to say, that's a lot of duties for one person.

And finally, to be the best product marketer you can be, you need to know 70 percent of everybody else's job so that you can work effectively and talk with authority. You should also work on your soft skills. We recommend pursuing self-development courses and finding a mentor. Don't just do what is expected of you in your workplace; think about your own development plan and what you need to do to achieve your goals.

The dream for any sole product marketer is to eventually build out an entire team of PMMs, but to do this, you have to be transparent from the get-go and demonstrate why the business should want to invest more money into employees like you. To do this, ensure you have consistent catch-ups and open communication when it comes to projects, revenue, and ops costs with either the financial team or the stakeholders directly. Something like a monthly/quarterly bulletin is a good start, but we would also recommend backing this up with face-to-face meetings too as it's often tricky to do your work justice when you're condensing it into a slide or two. Revenue obviously speaks for itself, but activities like customer feedback, to some people, might be viewed as unimportant. However, if you have a conversation, you can explain the importance behind it, share some verbatim quotes, and talk through what changes will be made on the back of them—and importantly, the business benefits of those changes.

So far, this has all been positioned with a view of you entering the company as a new starter. If you're the sole PMM at a company you've already been at for several months, or even years, and you're not getting the buy-in you deserve, it's not too late to follow the steps above. Just position them differently. So, instead of them being introductory, meet-and-greet-style sessions, say something like this to your stakeholders: "I'm strategizing for [insert time period] and would love to ensure your goals and challenges are being factored into those plans. It'd be great if we could schedule some time to chat about both of these in detail so I can go away and see how product marketing slots into both of these and provide some solutions."

When Robin Verderosa, Head of Product Marketing at Archipelago, joined a startup in the cryptocurrency space, she was the first marketing employee, but inevitably, down the line, she needed to expand the team. Upon reviewing the needs of the company with the CEO, it was decided it was time to scale up and hire a VP of Marketing, and this role soon became the senior leadership strategic role, and product marketing became more tactical.

To address concerns for maintaining a leadership position, she created a framework that she continues to follow to this day—and you can too.

First, meet with the major stakeholders early and often to understand their expectations. Once you've gotten buy-in on goals and specific projects, meet regularly to share updates, discuss obstacles, and update plans. Things are likely to change, so be flexible.

Second, create a go-to-market playbook and calendar that outlines the next six to twelve months of product launches and company initiatives. As product marketers, go-to-market isn't just about product launches as company milestones, industry events, and external influences; legal and regulatory guidelines need to be included in your go-to-market playbook. Partner with product management on your go-to-market to help validate the plan and create a bond with the product team that's seen as a two-way relationship.

Third, learn the product and technology really well; knowledge is power. You'll also save a lot of time by not having to seek out answers each time you tackle a new project. Make sure you can demo the product. This is a great opportunity to create your own demo script that you can share with sales if one doesn't already exist, or you can use it for your own purposes. Spend time with engineering to learn more about the technology, and make sure to have engineering literally draw out how it works, how one system interacts with another, and the processes and interdependencies. Remember to take pictures and keep them for reference.

Fourth, become an integral part of sales by setting up regular sales (training) meetings to share information on the product, competitors, industry, customers, and more. I prefer a biweekly meeting, but weekly or even monthly are okay. I also like to start the meeting on time and be considerate of everyone's schedule. Often, sales reps will be late due to client calls that are running late, but you'll want to avoid holding up the rest of the group. Make sure the VP of Sales attends the meetings so there are no qualms about the importance and value of the meeting. Come to each meeting with a clear agenda and make sure it's fast-paced and filled with valuable information.

Fifth, connect with your customers on a regular basis either through sales or through your own direct relationships. Start by understanding who your customers are. You may have had a hand in creating the personas, but now's the time to know just who those actual personas represent. You can do this by getting access to your CRM and using it daily to check reports, familiarize yourself with customers, and learn more about your prospects, including the size of the deal and where they are in the sales process. You'll also want to insist on listening in on sales calls as an active participant or at the very least as a fly on the wall. This will allow you to create relationships with customers for product feedback, case studies, and testimonials. The benefits of these relationships will pay off numerous times, especially as you're releasing new products, testing new messaging, and updating your website and your collateral. Armed with firsthand information about your customers and prospects, you'll be able to speak confidently about all aspects of the business including your customers, your market fit, competitors, revenue, forecasts, and feature requests. Don't forget to take what you hear back to the product team and other areas of the business.

The common thread with all five tenets is that they involve working with people throughout the organization. There are probably a few other relationship-building efforts that bring value to the role of product marketing that can be added or substituted in place of these. The most important takeaway is to just be mindful of product marketing's value within the organization and to not get sucked into the day-to-day tasks and lose your seat at the table.

## BUILDING A PRODUCT MARKETING FUNCTION

If you've done a great job and positioned yourself right as the sole PMM, your organization will ultimately make the wise decision to expand the team, and it will be partly up to you (as well as HR and the C-suite) to ensure the team is built intelligently. As you start building the team, it's not just about positioning yourself but positioning the other individuals within your team. You need to make sure that they know how to position themselves.

For instance, if you hire really junior people, they need to understand what they're hired to do, so that when they're having conversations or in meetings that you're not in, you're on the same page. You also need to ensure they're sufficiently up to speed on the ins and outs of your product(s) and customers. If you hire an associate product marketing manager and they're chatting with one of your product managers, and they are not clued up on expected details, this won't leave a great impression on (a) the individual and (b) the function, and as we all know, first impressions last.

When new people start, you need to do tours around the company. You can say, "This is this team now; this is how it's changed. This is what I'll be responsible for, this is what Richard will be responsible for, this is what Bryony is responsible for, etc." This will make it clear to people who they need to go to for what.

If new hires result in a change to the way your team is structured, be sure to clearly communicate this too. An example of this might be if previously you were the sole PMM, and you oversaw two products, but bringing in a new hire results in you overseeing one product and the new starter overseeing the second product. Be clear and vocal about the shifts within the team as it grows. This will make your teammates' lives so much easier as requests will get streamlined to the right person instead of being tossed around frustratingly. Doing this will add credibility to the whole department.

Everyone who joins the team needs to sit down with the heads of departments and have initial chats, even if they are very junior. You can't just tell them what happened in your one-on-ones as things may have changed in the weeks or months since you first arrived. Create an org chart for your team and keep it up to date, sharing it with other teams within the business so they can use it within their own onboarding processes. Having it written down as a one-pager (or recorded if you prefer) can be helpful as it can be referred to in the future.

*Top tip:* when growing your team, the skillset you need from your new PMM might be different from other members of the product marketing team, especially if you work for a company that has lots of different products. If, for instance, the PMM is going to be paired with a product manager who is excellent at pricing and packaging, you might want a PMM who is excellent at another aspect of the role, like content writing or customer interviews.

Likewise, if the product manager has a big weakness, you'd want a PMM who can excel in this area and take the lead. Obviously, you would want your new PMM to be competent in all areas so that if there is a reshuffle or their product manager leaves the organization, there's not a major skill deficit. But this can be a tricky ask.

How you scale your team will vary from company to company depending on what industry you're in, the makeup of your product portfolio, what your go-to-market and sales strategy looks like, the overall stage of the company, and probably many other factors. When Patrick Cuttica, former Director of Product Marketing at Sprout Social and now Senior Product Marketing Manager at Square, was building out the function at Sprout, in terms of role types and focus areas, the team structure unfolded like this:

- Product experts and go-to-market generalists
- General sales support (internal communications, lite enablement)
- Competitive/market intel
- Sales content
- Analyst relations

Moving forward, he also has his sights set on things like strategic customer insights, partner marketing, and pricing strategy/intel.

Patrick added:

> The key is understanding the core needs of your main stakeholders in Product, Sales, and Marketing. If you can identify the highest impact work across those groups (which can be difficult), then you can start to build a blueprint for how the various functions within the product marketing umbrella start to take shape.
>
> The important thing to keep in mind is to not bite off more than you can chew. It's easy for product marketing to be the catch-all for any content, strategy or initiative that the Product, Sales, and Marketing teams need supported. Be intentional in where you dedicate your time/effort and work with your stakeholders to prioritize which areas you can expand into as you grow.

There's a theory in psychology called the IKEA effect, which essentially says labor leads to love (i.e., if people help build something, they're more likely to like it than if it came premade). When building out your product marketing team, the same concept can be applied to your recruitment process. It's no secret product marketing is a highly cross-functional role, and whichever role your new recruit(s) slot into, one thing is for certain: they'll be working very closely with your product, marketing, and sales counterparts. If you bring each of these key stakeholders into a stage of your recruitment process and they feel like they have had a say in the hire, odds are, they're going to be more receptive to the new starter when they join, and this can only do wonders for how the two hit the ground running and how your team as a whole meshes with other departments. Better relationships equal more collaboration and cooperations, equals better outcomes, equals better perception of product marketing.

When Div Manickam, Portfolio Messaging and Platform Evangelist, grew her product marketing team threefold (from four to twelve) in her last role, her interview process looked like this:

1. Recruiter screening (30 minutes)
2. PMM team member screening (30–45 minutes) for technical aptitude/PMM skillset
3. PMM leader screening (30 minutes) for cultural fit
4. Presentation and Q&A (45 minutes) to the panel across product marketing, product management, sales engineering, and marketing communications

As well as testing for skills fit, testing for a candidate's cultural fit is also essential. Having a revolving door of product marketing members starting and leaving is no good for anyone. You'll throw an awful lot of wasted time, money, and productivity down the drain. It can also tarnish your reputation if others in the company start to think you can't bring in great team members, as well as the department's reputation if PMMs start to be seen as "flaky."

Going back to Div's recruitment process, she would ask each candidate if the values below resonated. For Div, this became a good litmus test and made it easier to know who genuinely believed in these values with anecdotes of their own.

### PMM TEAM VALUES AND BELIEFS

**Inspire: Trust and Credibility**
*We trust and respect each other, irrespective of level.*

**Influence: Extreme Ownership**
*We own what we do: the good, bad, and ugly,
and are accountable to each other.*

**Impact: Results and Relationships**
*We strive for team recognition, not individual
recognition—we win or lose together.*

These values and beliefs may differ for your team, but the principle still applies.

Before we move on to the next section, here are a couple of final nuggets for when you're building out your product marketing function.

The first comes from Phill Agnew, Senior Product Marketing Manager at Hotjar. He says, "Great PMMs I've worked with aren't just brilliant at the tactical part of their role. They're also brilliant at getting the most out of the people they work with. I've seen PMMs level up their teams by hosting workshops that engage people, making teammates feel welcome and trusted, while keeping the group moving forward. PMMs that take time to improve their collaboration skills, to take ownership of projects, and lead initiatives will find it far easier to climb the career ladder."

The takeaway: enabling and enthusing your team is essential for growth in every aspect.

And finally, when we asked Kim Pfluger, Director of Product Marketing and Program Management at Valimail, how she coaches and encourages members of the PMM team, her top tips were:

- Ask more than you convince. You'll learn more and you listen more. Not every conversation has to have an agenda.
- If something feels unnatural, scary, or difficult, lean in. You're growing.
- You can always use customer data to break a tie.

- Don't be afraid to have an alternative opinion or ask a scary question—you're unlikely to be the only one who's thinking that way.
- Product development is messy. Embrace the chaos.
- Lean on your team—everyone has different strengths and blind spots. It's okay to ask for help.

For Kim, these have not only helped in growing her own career but also in "unsticking" her teams from inaction, fear, or doubt.

## WHERE SHOULD YOUR TEAM SIT?

There's an awful lot of debate around who product marketing should report to: product or marketing. As we mentioned in our predictions for the future earlier in the book, someday soon, we anticipate product marketing will be a department of its own, reporting directly to the CEO. For now, though, the majority ladder into either product or marketing.

In reality, there is no right or wrong, and each has its pros and cons. For Mark Assini, Product Marketing Manager at Voices. com, PMM sits within the marketing organization alongside demand-gen, content, and communications. The pros to this include effective positioning and messaging alignment across all marketing functions; strong coordination of content and demand generation efforts during product releases or launches; and generally more creative thinking, given the inherent creative nature of marketing as a function and department. On the flip side, the cons include requiring more time and effort to ensure effective alignment and communication between product marketing, product, and sales departments; a tendency to over-index on communications of product releases and launches; and reduced input on the product roadmap.

If you report into marketing and feel you're getting limited exposure to the product roadmap early on, you should go above and beyond to build a great relationship with the product team by having weekly stand-ups and twice-daily desk stops (or the virtual equivalent if you work remotely) to make sure you're still getting what you need from the team you're not sitting in. This can be applied the opposite way too—if you sit in product, you won't be as close to marketing, so you'll need to work hard to get alignment.

Don't skimp on this. Product and marketing are critical to your success, and lack of collaboration with either can be a huge detriment to your success and ultimately, performance and perception. Be very intentional with your communication, be thoughtful about how you position product marketing, have explicit role clarity, and clearly define where the handoff point is for any given responsibility or initiative.

## HOW PRODUCT MARKETING TEAMS SHOULD BE ORGANIZED

The structure of the product marketing team can vary greatly from one company to the next. There are typically four structures—with each having its own pros and cons. Let's take a look.

### By Feature

This is arguably the easiest way of structuring a product marketing team. Each product marketer is paired up with one or more product manager(s). The ideal PM to PMM ratio is generally considered to be 2:1, but it depends on the size of your company and what you want to accomplish as to whether this would suit you.

This structure allows good communication between PM and PMM and makes responsibilities clear as everyone is in their mini-team. However, when you structure by features, the features tend to take center stage, rather than the customers. This can be a big drawback.

If you are structured by feature, you need to position yourself as the expert on that feature. You need to know everything about it. This will result in people coming to you about that feature and you knowing the answers. You shouldn't need to ask someone else.

### By Function

When you structure a team by function, you split them into four columns:

- Market intelligence
- Messaging and positioning
- Launch and go-to-market strategy
- Sales enablement

This often is not a very effective way of structuring a team as each sub-team is working independently. It doesn't allow you to work as strategically as you could.

If you are structured by function, make sure you're the expert on your specific pillar, and everyone else knows it. You want to be the central source of truth.

When Sapphire Reels, Senior Product Marketing Manager at Pluralsight (a 1,600-plus employee company) originally started, the team was "full-stack product marketers"—each owning some of the four pillars of market intel, positioning and messaging, launch and go-to-market strategy, and sales enablement. She says it was fine at first, but as the team scaled, the setup created a ton of inefficiency. She says, "We had one product at that time, but we have many product teams who own feature sets, and we were paired with a team. It was hard to have a cohesive launch strategy. We also became stretched thin, as some folks started to specialize just by nature of their strengths. We were a very project-based team at the time."

They then saw an opportunity to reorganize, and now the team has:

- A Product Squad that focuses on the four pillars of PMM. At Pluralsight, this is specifically for products (i.e., people don't do general competitive intelligence; they only do it for their assigned product set). This was enabled by the fact that their product teams also reorganized. Sapphire now supports a set of product teams focused on one persona as well as our PaaS (platform as a service) team.

- A Sales Squad that is focused on the sales relationship and working with the sales enablement team.
- A GTM Squad that focuses on scaling sales and marketing plays.

They're still relatively new with this organization and trying to figure out what it means, but this is their current thinking as an example for a launch:

> The product squad works with the product team to get the products ready for launch. We build the launch story, which is then turned over to the GTM squad. The GTM squad builds out the GTM story based on our launch story, and then the GTM sales play manager and GTM marketing play manager both facilitate the campaigns and needs across those teams. The sales squad would provide support for the sales plays.

### By Line of Business

If you sell to different buyers within one company, this approach is often ideal. It is a customer-focused model in which you align yourself to marketing, finance, and sales, etc. Be the authority in this area, get time with the product team so you understand the product inside out, learn about its technical features and what other products are on the market.

For Jenkin Lee, Chief Product Officer at Baze, being organized by line of business or product area has typically been his preference, and a PM, PMM, and the associated engineering team would work together as a unit to release feature iterations.

The biggest pro to this approach is the product-culture alignment and shared team empathy around release goals. The biggest challenge is that often in larger companies where engineering might report to a CTO and PMM up to the CMO, there are other siloed team goals and individual objectives that get in the way of those shared goals.

Jenkin added, "Getting the team structure to work in this newer/ nontraditional setup has always been the hardest part. At Baze, I happen to lead Product, Marketing, and Engineering, so driving alignment is much easier."

### By Objective or Theme

When you structure by objective or theme, you align your resources to the biggest need of the company at a particular time. You can focus on big launches for part of the year and switch to other key areas at other times.

This type of team structure does need product marketers who are excellent at all four disciplines and requires a lot of coordination within the team. You don't have time to do everything, so you have to prioritize.

Organizing your team for impact is essential to the integrity of the product marketing role. For example, if you opt to organize by objective or theme, but the PMMs in your team aren't all-rounders, you're not necessarily set up for success, and this could bite you in the rear. Or, if you restructure to organize by feature, you have to be 100 percent confident that before that restructure takes place, each PMM is an absolute expert on that feature. If they're not, this will become apparent very quickly and will not reflect well on your team.

Analyze your team's strengths and weaknesses and plot backwards from there. And remember, there's not necessarily a one-size-fits-all approach when it comes to team structures. If there's an out-of-the-box structure that works for you and the rest of your company, run with it.

## THE FIVE KEY PERSONAS

What's your personality type?

Yoni Solomon, former Director of Product Marketing at G2, now CMO at Uptime.com, believes there are five different personas. When it comes to pitching your role in different stage companies, he recommends positioning your role around the needs of the company, and by his count, there are five different "types" or personas of product marketers: Storytellers (expert positioners), Performers (expert trainers), Evangelists (product experts),

Strategists (expert campaign launchers), and Playmakers (expert revenue generators).

Each is based around the core skills and competencies PMMs bring to the table, and Yoni's advice is to lean into the persona your company most needs you to be.

For example, an early-stage company might need a strong Storyteller, whose responsibility it is to define the narrative of the new category their company is trying to establish.

On the other hand, another company that just raised its Series A is now ramping up sales and marketing—which means they'll need a strong Performer, Strategist, and Playmaker to enable the people-facing teams and launch campaigns to drive adoption.

Another company that perhaps offers a complex technical solution—or sits in a highly regulated industry—might need a serious Evangelist who understands the nuances of the product and industry well enough to translate it for the rest of the org.

The key is to build a strong PMM toolkit of skills, which will allow you to essentially "become" exactly the type of product marketer your company needs at that specific time or stage.

Once you've built your repertoire, molding yourself into *exactly* what your company needs will effectively illustrate the diversity of your skillset, show how you add value at various stages of growth, and quickly get others in the org to see how integral you are in all these different scenarios.

Take a look at Yoni's descriptions of each of the five personas' core skills and signature outputs below. Which do you most relate to?

### Meet the Storyteller

- **Core Skill:** expert value, story architect
- **Best Understands:** our buyers and their problems
- **Signature Output:** killer message houses, target personas
- **Applicable KPIs:** MQLs and top funnel demand
- **Background:** creative writing and advertising

### Meet the Performer

- **Core Skill:** expert in-person storyteller
- **Best Understands:** how people-facing teams best learn about products
- **Signature Output:** strong GTM enabler of sales orgs
- **Applicable KPIs:** GTM certification, time to first deal
- **Background:** theatre, music, public speaking, and education

### Meet the Evangelist

- **Core Skill:** ultimate product expert
- **Best Understands:** simplifying complex solutions for all to understand
- **Signature Output:** user guides, FAQs, objections

- **Applicable KPIs:** product satisfaction, feedback capture, beta management
- **Background:** customer success, solution consultant, or product

### Meet the Strategist
- **Core Skill:** bringing GTM concepts to life
- **Best Understands:** tactics to launch new products and capabilities
- **Signature Output:** campaigns, segments, workflows
- **Applicable KPIs:** pipeline ops created/influenced
- **Background:** growth manager, ops, or project management

### Meet the Playmaker
- **Core Skill:** expert revenue generator (and reporter)
- **Best Understands:** how your sales cycle operates, and when it's best to launch
- **Signature Output:** sales org collab, win/loss, new markets, competitive
- **Applicable KPIs:** closed/won new biz, renewal, upsell
- **Background:** SDR/sales, business operations, or enablement

# CHAPTER 4

# THE PRODUCT IS KING

When it comes to making important decisions and strategies on marketing budgets, pricing, and roadmaps, the product life cycle is key to both company owners and whole marketing teams.

In this section of the book, we will:

- Think about the role of product marketing throughout the product life cycle.
- Review the buyer journey and why it matters.
- Discuss how to pitch your role at different stage companies.

## WHAT STAGE IS THE PRODUCT AT?

It's very important to spend time thinking about the role and value of product marketing throughout the product life cycle.

Broadly speaking, there are five stages within any product's life cycle:

- Development
- Introduction
- Growth
- Maturity
- Decline

You need to be familiar with these cycles because the stage the product is in will heavily influence your role and goals.

## DEVELOPMENT STAGE

During this initial stage, you and other business areas will research, develop, and test new products or features before they are introduced. This phase is instrumental. Money will be spent without any returns because the product isn't available to buy. Depending on the product, this stage might last a long time.

Your goal in this phase is to be the voice of the research. Have weekly or biweekly meetings (depending on how much data you're collecting) with key stakeholders to cascade your findings down. Let them know what the action points are, and have a clear line of communication. Understand the data so that when people ask you questions about it, you're not caught off guard. If any questions do prove difficult to answer, don't try and blag your way through it as this can cause a lot of damage to your reputation. Just say, "Let me get back to you after the meeting."

Always lead with data, not opinions. Provide evidence (customer calls are great for this).

Your role will involve:

- Being the voice of the customer and the market.
- Finding out what target customers want by speaking to them.
- Analyzing the competitive landscape.
- Defining what your customers' must-have requirements are.
- Collaborating with other teams on messaging.

By the end of this stage, you should have a very clear understanding of who your target market is and what their needs are, as well as an in-depth understanding of the product or feature itself. Sit down with your product counterpart and go through your market findings together so you both understand fully and have a good grounding.

Phill Agnew, Senior Product Marketing Manager at Hotjar, says, "Product marketing in my organization is intensely important at the early stages of a product life cycle. With so much ambiguity about what problems you're looking to solve, what personas to target, and even what features to build, a PMM has a vital role in gathering information and informing the business. A great PMM will help the organization focus on building a solution that will provide the most value to the market."

## INTRODUCTION STAGE

This begins as soon as your product or feature is made available to the market. It's important to test, test, and test some more in the introduction phase, resolving any issues before you spend big on marketing campaigns. You need to be central to the key initiatives. This will ensure you are in a much stronger position when you have your hard launch and release it to the masses. It should save you a lot of money too.

The aim of this phase is to make sure you have the best possible version of your product and its positioning. Your role will involve:

- Identifying the right buyer persona.
- Looking at how people are reacting to the product (i.e., do they find value?).
- Finding out what they like and dislike.
- Comparing the product with competitor alternatives.
- Discovering if people have any worries or concerns with the product.
- Seeing if there are any customer needs that aren't being met.
- Educating potential customers.
- Orchestrating the product/solution launch.

It's a communication game. A lot of this phase is still research. Communicate your personas, your competitive intel, and any new trends. Explain to your colleagues what they need to do with this; otherwise, they might turn around and say, "So what?" Share the action plan, the takeaways.

## GROWTH STAGE

The middle phase of the product life cycle is growth, and this is when you'll see demand growing and sales coming in. At this stage, it's more about understanding revenue—how much is coming in, where it's coming from, company expectations and forecasts, and where product marketing can help. For instance, if the marketing team is 20 percent below target, you can make suggestions based on your knowledge of the current revenue streams. For example: "Why don't we try and segment by this data or use this persona, and see if it helps you hit our target?" Or if sales are struggling to hit quota, do they need any additional sales assets created? If you come in with an action plan to help them hit their revenue target, you'll buy yourself a ton of credibility and elevate your function internally.

This phase will have a heavy focus around revenue, but according to our research, 50 percent of product marketers aren't targeted against generating new revenue. The career path for director or VP-level product marketers is to chief marketer officer roles, so if you fall into the 50 percent who are potentially distant from the revenue side of things, we'd suggest being proactive and getting closer. Having a really solid grounding and understanding of marketing will add another layer to how people think of you, and you'll be able to have higher-level, strategic conversations.

In this phase, you'll spend the majority of your marketing activity's budget, while continually tweaking, refining, and improving what you're currently doing in terms of both promotions and your actual product. You are shifting strategy and execution to derive value by adding features and capabilities.

The market and competition will change during this phase, and that means perceptions will too. You must keep on top of both what customers want and what competitors are doing and change your strategy accordingly. You should ask yourself:

- Is our messaging still resonating?
- Is the unique value of our product clear despite the competitive landscape?
- Are our customers desperate for new features?
- Are we searching for customers in the right places?

Your marketing campaigns will evolve during this stage, shifting from getting customers to desire and purchase the product, to communications pushing why your brand is better than your competitors'.

## MATURITY STAGE

The penultimate phase is maturity, and this is where sales will begin to plateau. Your role is now to try to maintain your market share and industry authority. There will usually be lots of competing products at this stage, so it is more difficult to maintain market share. Now is the time to think about how you can reinvent your business model. Can you offer something that others can't? Can you cross-sell to existing customers?

Mature companies often fall into the status quo trap. They avoid risk and suffocate innovation by continuing to work on projects that have historically delivered results. As a PMM, your job is to show how your consumers are changing and make sure you're still relevant for their needs, and that can involve making changes.

Find out what customers want *now*—their opinions will have changed since the introductory stage. The information you glean needs to be passed on to the product teams so they can look at adding new features or developing a new product. You may be able to enter new market segments to increase your revenue stream in verticals your competitors perhaps aren't already actively targeting. This stage is all about seizing opportunities and taking calculated risks to do something that'll make you really stand out from the crowd. Be creative and try to find a different way to differentiate yourself. Use your data and your customer calls to come up with plans and strategies. If you come up with a strategy that differentiates you and delivers meaningful revenue impact, it's going to work absolute wonders for your positioning. You just need to approach the right people with the right ideas, be innovative, and push the boundaries.

For Div Manickam, Portfolio Messaging (Product, Industry, and Solutions) and Platform Evangelist, customer case studies and advocacy programs are key to drive retention and lead to referrals once a product reaches maturity. Her mature customers are the biggest advocates and superheroes who share success stories at annual conferences.

## DECLINE STAGE

Products can decline for a number of reasons. Maybe there's no longer a need for them—like the way physical media like CDs, DVDs, Blu-rays, and books are being replaced by streaming and digital options. Perhaps customers' needs have changed, or technology has moved on, or perhaps the product itself wasn't up to scratch.

During the decline phase, sales start to drop, and this phase probably relies on product marketing the least because marketing budgets are usually reduced. However, you will want to be at the table to understand and drive decisions and their execution so that you can help build the discontinuation and deprecation plan.

In this stage, you may want to consider implementing price cuts, which could impact how you position your product. Alternatively, you can think of another use for your product—which would involve a big positioning and messaging overhaul and a whole new set of customer research and analysis, effectively resetting the product cycle. Finally, you can wait for the demand to come back, get acquired by another company, or just discontinue the product full stop. Not every product marketer will necessarily see this phase, and in an ideal world, the work you and other key business areas do will prevent the product decline phase in the first place.

## PITCHING YOUR ROLE AT
## DIFFERENT-STAGE COMPANIES

Early-stage startups can hugely benefit from making a product marketer their first marketing hire—we might seem biased, but in many ways, it's a no-brainer. If a company doesn't have the results from essential product marketing work—like customer research, positioning, messaging, enablement, and so on, their marketing campaigns are not set up for success. You need to target the right people, with the right message, at the right time, and a PMM plays a key part in unpacking this. This isn't just limited to the marketing team's efforts either; it applies to the conversations sales reps are having, and customer success too. And of course, the product marketing role is equally important as the company begins to establish itself.

We caught up with Dan Murphy, VP of Marketing at Privy, about how the product marketing role evolves throughout the stages. During his career tenure to date, Dan has experienced all three stages: early-stage, growth-stage, and multi-product stage. He started his career in HubSpot's product marketing team, around three years away from an IPO. After HubSpot, he worked in a really small startup called OnShape, where he grew the company (with the freemium model) from beta to thirty thousand signups a month. Dan then took a role at Drift, which was pretty early-stage when he joined, but over the two and a half years he was there, the team scaled from three people to thirty and grew revenue ten times. Drift went from selling one product to four products and by the end, they were supporting more than sixty sales reps, a customer team of about thirty, and well over ninety on the product team between product management, engineering, and designers, etc. Most recently, Dan joined Privy, a small startup in the e-commerce space (an e-commerce marketing platform), which also has a big freemium funnel, and here Dan oversees brand, content, and product marketing.

Encapsulating all his experience, here is Dan's take on product marketing through the three stages:

| Stage | Early-stage company | Growth-stage company | Multi-product company |
|---|---|---|---|
| Focus | Function-based:<br>• Product launches<br>• Product content<br>• Product education | Customer-based:<br>• Product messaging<br>• Product success<br>• Product enablement | Project-based:<br>• Multi-product story<br>• Solutions marketing<br>• Verticals |
| Goal | Find product/market fit | Find feature/customer fit | Find product/ segment fit |

$$\longrightarrow \text{Knowledge}$$

As your company grows, your product marketing team becomes more of a knowledge center and less of a function-based team.

## EARLY-STAGE COMPANY

The focus for product marketing in an early-stage company is more function-based work such as launches, creating product content, and product education. The overall goal is to find the product-market fit, which is also the company's goal.

You'll learn so much from this function-based work. The team won't be investing in marketing until they figure out how they can rationalize that investment. So, you're probably the sole product marketer. At this stage, there has to be an obvious output of your work—it may be marketing qualified leads (MQLs), or it may be project-based work.

### Areas of Focus

- **Product launches:** launching something monthly (as Dan tried to do at Drift every single month, putting a ton of marketing momentum behind it) to keep your audience engaged
- **Early customer proof:** case studies, quotes, tweets, recognizable logos (big brands who are validating your product), and videos
- **Product content:** use cases, integrations, demo videos, webinars
- **Product story:** a deck or video pitch to help get everyone singing the same tune
- **Competitive intel:** having a resource with basic objection handling for the sales team

When Privy launched a new tool that helps customers cross-sell, Dan did a video on cross-selling and a webinar on cross-selling. He did a video on YouTube about it and a blog post. He also worked on a help doc and created a paper trail of content specific to a use case that the team knew would be valuable. It was instantly validated as something their customers wanted when they launched it because of the amount of email responses they got, people sharing their blog post, commenting on their video, joining their webinar, etc. It was very, very obvious quickly that the content was a hit.

When it comes to the product story, have a really tight deck. A video pitch will really help get everybody singing the same tune in your company, whether it's sales, customer success, or your management team. Have a three-minute video with the deck explaining the product pitch and what problems you are solving.

## GROWTH-STAGE COMPANY

With a growth-stage company, it's more customer-based. There's a lot more work to be done on messaging, identifying product success, positioning, and enablement across different teams. The role is more about finding features and customer fit. You'll have product-market fit and understand the market, so now you have to understand the magic: why it matches the market.

This stage is about trying to better understand what features your customers are using and why they love those features. Most customers will not use every feature, so digging in here is really important.

Now that your company is bigger, it will have established teams that own customer relationships, demand generation, sales, and product development. Instead of product marketing producing its own content or doing more function-based work, you'll now transition to enabling the rest of the organization.

There's a lot of enablement with sales, customer success, marketing, and product teams that you can be doing. And you're probably spending even more time talking to customers, testing messaging within the org, and training other teams.

Dan shared a case study:

> A good example of this is a tool called Gong that we used at Drift. It was really helpful for us because what it does is it records all sales and customer success calls. So, every call is automatically recorded. It gives us a big library, and in the library, we can search for keywords and stuff that was spoken on the calls, which is extremely powerful to product marketers, because now we can go in and we can research features, we can research different segments, and connect with Salesforce.

> We can look at highly precise lists of customers that we want to know more about. It was really, really helpful for us to be able to dig in and understand our customers better. I think our team listened to more calls on Gong than any other team, which was pretty awesome.

## Areas of Focus

- **Customer success enablement**: onboarding decks, business reviews, industry/market training, and new feature training
- **Product messaging**: researching customer feedback and market trends (one of the biggest focuses at this stage)
- **Product tour**: telling your product story on your website (videos, infographics), making your number one sales rep (your website) precision perfect
- **Sales enablement**: training your sales team, product marketing SLA, intel, and distribution of it.
- **Market or analysis proof**: investing in third-party or expert validation

When you focus on these, you can test out a lot of messages, and you can train your teams on it. And then with Gong, you can actually go back and make sure they were talking about the right stuff. You can also understand how your customers reacted and understand how your own team did the training.

You are being a little bit less functional or tactical and being a little bit more strategic. You're spending more of your time becoming a knowledge center. You're spending more time researching and understanding the customers in the market.

## MULTI-PRODUCT COMPANY

This stage is more product-based, and during it, you will focus on the multi-product story, and you will likely be doing solutions marketing. You might also be experimenting with verticals and finding different products and segments and how they fit.

Product marketing must focus on being able to tell the multi-product story, or each product's individual story. The focus is on the new market or segment penetration, and product marketing should lead that effort with research and providing understanding.

In this stage, a lot of product marketing teams will be heavily involved in pricing and packaging. As such, in telling the story, Dan suggests bucketing pricing and packaging as part of that. Also focus on new market or segment penetration. This is almost going full circle, and now you're back to that early stage where you were trying to find product-market fit. Now you have new products you've got to understand. Do your existing segments like this new product? Are they the right fit for it? What is the positioning for them? How do you use those two products together? How do you use them individually? Is it a new segment? There are different questions you must answer in this stage, and you should hopefully be creating really tight feedback loops with your executive team.

### Areas of Focus

- **Multi-product story**: why each product is uniquely suited to provide value and why they are even better together
- **Solutions marketing**: pairing PMM resources with business units or segments

- **Customer and market insights**: creating fast feedback loops between your customers or the market and your executive team
- **Company enablement**: across all departments, distribution of product information and positioning

Big thank you to Dan for sharing his invaluable insights on this!

# CHAPTER 5

# FIRST IMPRESSIONS COUNT

To hit the ground running in any company, and at any level, you need to focus on building key relationships early on so you can extract the information needed to effectively demonstrate your value in the future.

In this section of the book, we will:

- Focus on what to find out when you're new at a company.
- Look at the importance of research (whether you're new or have been in the role for a while).
- List the key questions to ask key members of each team.
- Show you how to devise internal personas.

## GETTING OFF TO THE BEST START

When you join a new company, you need to learn where you fit before you can make any kind of impact. You're probably used to doing extensive customer research—now it's time to research your internal counterparts.

In the first two weeks, you should schedule time to speak to your senior managers, your chief product officer, chief marketing officer, chief strategy officer, chief revenue officer, etc. To set the right foundation straight away, ask them what they want from you, how you can help them, how they want to communicate, how they want to work with you, what their current pain points are, and so on. Your manager will be best placed to tell you who the most critical stakeholders are for product marketing.

You might find people are more open with you and will tell you what they're thinking with fewer reservations because you're a new person. This gives you a great opportunity to get to the heart of problems quickly and look at challenges with fresh eyes. You may even be able to suggest solutions that are more creative than someone who's been in the job for years because you're less fixed in how you think about the company and the product.

That said, if you have been in a company for a year or more and you haven't done the get-to-know-you step, it is still important to do it now. Not having sound internal research will limit your effectiveness no matter how long you've been in the role. Start putting in some meetings with stakeholders and understanding what is happening, almost as if you are starting new. Make sure you position why you're having the meetings—as it won't be obvious. Say something like, "You know, we are revisiting some of our priorities for product marketing, so I'd love to take the opportunity to sit with different team members and learn about what's working and what's not working."

You need to work with people how they want to be worked with. For example, your CMO and CEO will want different things from you; they'll want to communicate in different ways, and it's really important to grasp this. If you don't, it will cause friction and lead to problems—and that's not productive for *anyone*.

By having meetings with the key people in different departments, you'll be able to use the information you glean to understand how to deliver value to each specific team. For example, your sales teams aren't going to want the same things as your product teams, and your customer service teams will have different needs as well. It's up to you to learn their requirements of product marketing, and then work to meet those requirements in a mutually conducive way.

YOUR ACTION PLAN

- **Action point #1**: If you're new to a company, do your research. Make a list of all the people you need to speak to, and start booking out time in people's calendars.

- **Action point #2:** If you've been at a company for a while and already had conversations with key stakeholders, ask yourself a few questions: How long ago did you have these meetings? Is the information you gleaned from them still accurate? Have priorities changed? Have internal structures or job roles changed? Are there new/different stakeholders who you should have a relationship with?

- **Action point #3:** If you've already been through this process and are going through it again, before you head into the meeting, write up your notes/takeaways from the last time you had this conversation. This will show that you're prepared and that you listen, and it will enable you to easily see what has changed.

## CREATE PERSONAS

This process doesn't stop there. You will need to break down your findings further and think about the different personalities in each team. As a product marketer, you'll be used to creating profiles of the people who buy or use your products. Now, you must use the same skills to create internal personas for your stakeholders outside of product marketing. This will help you market yourself to people within each department more effectively. Think about things like their personality traits, their objectives, their wants and needs, internal and external challenges, and the size and structure of their teams.

You can then use this information to create a one-pager on each key person. This will help you immensely, especially if you work for a big organization, because you can look at these sheets before meetings to remind yourself of the personality traits of the people who will be in attendance. One way of looking at these one-pagers is that they're like the personality assessment tests you sometimes have to fill out when you apply for a job.

Once you have these personas, you can tailor everything to suit your internal audience. For example, if one person loves detail and wants to know the ins and outs of everything, they would love a twenty-slide deck to go through events. Others might want a five-minute phone call or a quick email with a few bullet points instead.

Here is an example one-pager:

**Name:** Bryony
**Title:** Head of Content and Education
**Department:** Marketing
**Team Structure:** Bryony manages eight internal copywriters.
**Objectives:**
- Ensuring the company's content strategy obtains MoM growth and is always in line with what customers want and one step ahead of the competition
- Building out and launching innovative products—both paid for and free—that solve problems for product marketers

- Driving sales across the company's portfolio of products through tactical and strategic marketing campaigns

**Pain Points:**
- Managing multiple simultaneous products and campaigns across several community lines
- Measuring the success of individual releases

**Communication Preferences:** Bryony prefers either in-person meetings or phone calls. She's to-the-point and will always opt for a numbers-led approach, where possible.

## FROM PERSONA TO PERSONALITY TESTS

Personality tests are another way of really understanding your key colleagues, and did you know, more than 88 percent of Fortune 500 companies[1] now use personality tests as part of the hiring process? If you haven't done one yet, you'll probably be in the minority. Some of the most popular are the Myers–Briggs Type Indicator (MBTI), Enneagram, DiSC, and Caliper Profile.

Personality tests can help hugely during the hiring process when trying to decide which candidate would fit better into the existing team and company culture. They can also be useful long term as they can indicate how someone will react to situations,

---

1 The Myers–Briggs Company, https://www.themyersbriggs.com/en-US/Products-and-Services/Myers-Briggs

which personality types they will gel with (or not), how they perceive and process information, and how best to communicate with them.

G2's CMO Ryan Bonnici grew his marketing team from five to around sixty-five in a year. He's joked that that time was "utter hell," and that he "wouldn't advise it," but it was worth it to find the talent he wanted so they could target other audiences.

Having so many people join the marketing team within a year could have caused issues, but thanks to personality tests, Ryan was able to create a harmonious working environment. On everyone's laptop is a sticker that displays their personality test results—what sort of interaction they like, etc. This means that when people approach them, they know how to interact with them to get better results.

Whether you go for personas, personality tests, or both, the byproduct is stronger relationships. Think about it: the same way you send targeted and tailored marketing messages to customers to strengthen the customer-to-company relationship, personalizing your approach internally enhances your PMM-to-stakeholder relationships.

## SHOW YOUR VALUE

Hosting initial meetings and building trust in each department, unfortunately, isn't enough. You also need to show them what value you're going to bring to each team. It's a thankless task but must be done if you want to be an effective product marketer.

Use the defining product-marketing slide deck from Chapter 1 and show it at these meetings. With the slide deck, you'll be able to show what you are here to do, what you have achieved in your previous companies, and how you can help each department hit their specific targets/achieve their goals. Even if you have been at the company for six months or more, the slide deck is still a great tool. You can highlight some of the great work you and your teammates have achieved in your time with the company, and how it has impacted the department you're presenting to.

In an ideal world, these meetings would happen face to face. Having a conversation in a room with someone allows you to build a better relationship than a conversation over email. If you are working from home or work in a different state, face to face meetings might not be an option for you—so try and have video calls rather than a standard phone call. You want them to feel like they're getting to know you, and seeing your face is essential for this. You'll also be able to read their body language and dig into things together, further building a connection.

Before you go into any initial "getting to know you" meeting, it can be useful to be prepared with a list of questions you want to ask.

We've put together our favorites to get you started. Take a few minutes to highlight or underline the questions that are most relevant to you, and don't be afraid to add your own. (Definitely don't ask every question, or your meetings will feel like an interrogation, and you'll end up burning bridges rather than building them!)

KEY QUESTIONS TO ASK

### General

- What do you expect from me, so I can help you succeed?
- What are you primarily responsible for?
- How would you like us to work together?
- What are you excited about right now?
- What aspect of your job do you dread at the moment?
- What were you most proud of last year, and how can you better it?
- How do you define success?
- What challenges stand in the way of you getting your job done/hitting your targets?
- Who else should I speak to?
- Do you ever feel restricted in what you are able to do?
- What are your team's goals?
- What are your three biggest problems/stresses at the moment?

### Sales

- What are your team's objectives?
- What are your current barriers to those objectives?
- How have you worked with product marketing in the past?

- What key obstacle stops you from selling more?
- What are your top-performing reps doing that your others are not?
- What kind of feedback do your reps get from lost deals?
- What keeps you up at night?

### Product Team

- Where do you think the line of product marketing and product management should begin and end?
- What's your utopia vision for how we'll work together moving forward?
- What are your biggest pain points right now, and how do you think we can help break them down?
- What is something that's missing right now?
- What would you like the product marketing team to focus on more?

### CEO

- How do you envision product marketing slotting in with the wider organization?
- What impact would you like product marketing to have?
- What gaps does the company have, and how can product marketing help fill them?
- How will/would you measure product marketing's impact?
- What do you see as the company's biggest barriers over the next twelve months?
- What is the company's biggest strength?
- What is the company's biggest weakness?

**Marketing**

- What is the marketing team measured on?
- How do you think product marketing can help you meet those goals?
- What kind of activities do you usually partner with product marketing on?
- What are your most successful channels to date?
- What are your plans for the next quarter?
- What does your relationship with product and sales look like?

## CREATE ALLIES IN PRODUCT

There is a popular notion that product managers "put the product on the shelf," and product marketers "get the product off the shelf" by driving go-to-market strategy.

But this is a misconception and hugely undervalues the involvement of a product marketer. A product marketer's work begins much earlier than a product getting to the shelf.

The way product marketing teams and product teams interact will vary considerably from company to company, but whatever it is like in your company, you must build close-knit relationships with your product counterparts to give yourself a solid foundation.

We can't stress how fundamental the relationship with product management is to your success as a product marketer. Pendo's

Director of Product Marketing, Marcus Andrews, has eight great tips to share:

1. **Understand your product:** be a technical expert, know customer use cases of your product, have a strong demo game (you could jump on a sales call, jump on a support call and do just as good a job as any salesperson/PM), and speak fluent PM (you know every feature in detail). The PM team knows you know your stuff because you're putting a lot of effort in.

2. **Learn the roadmap:** know the future product (what it is today and what it will be in the future), help paint that vision through your creative skills, defer to them rather than trying to dictate the product roadmap, and write about it to bring the vision to life (i.e., a memo or a press release can really help your PMs).

3. **Understand their goals:** know a product's goals, help set shared goals as a team so you have goal alignment, and build a shared vision.

4. **Meet regularly:** get to know them as individuals, ask questions, get them excited, and communicate in a way that works for both of you (i.e., a weekly meeting/Slack/in person).

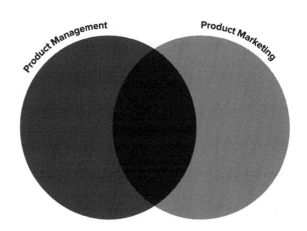

**Product development and product marketing collaboration**

Product Management

Product Marketing

5. **Set clear expectations:** demonstrate value/impact early and often to build trust, build an equal partnership (don't think that you work for the PM etc.; you're all supporting the product, and the customers that use the product are the boss), make them aware to share (they won't have 100 percent of your time, all the time), and treat all your PMs equally; don't have favorites.

6. **Learn the market:** PM owns the problem they're solving for the customers, PMM owns the market. You're the experts when it comes to competitors, trends you're seeing, topics, etc. Deliver market insights/personas.

7. **Give them the narrative:** develop the story with your PMs and really involve them. Help them with words; they

might write something super technical, but you can make it more straightforward/easier to read.

8. **Be product driven**: become the voice of product outside of product and engineering, and push the marketing team to be more product driven to ultimately solve for the customer.

The product team will be one of the core internal departments that you have the most interaction with. Gwendolyn Smith, Senior Manager, Product Marketing at a leading software company, explains: "We talk to the product team all day long, join their sprint reviews, and have a seat at the table for product council. Focused one-on-one time comes in the form of biweekly meetings as we align on market intel, release strategy, messaging, and promotions."

You must do all you can to make a good first impression if you are new to a company. If you have been with your company for a while and you don't have a great relationship with the product team already, perhaps you should make it one of your priorities. You won't be able to thrive and do a good job if you are at loggerheads. You need to get them to understand how valuable you are and that you can help them—especially in areas such as market validation, user research, strategy and business case, product growth/adoption, and user onboarding/journeys.

You need to get the balance right, with both teams understanding where you overlap and where you pass over.

**Product Marketing**

- Represents the voice of the customer—before, during, and after launch
- **Is responsible for the positioning and messaging of new products and features in line with market demands**
- Defines key value props of new and updated products
- **Works closest with sales and product management**
- Drives product adoption and advocacy

**Product Management**

- Focuses on developing and defining a product
- **Is responsible for setting the product roadmap and the product vision**
- Identifes customer pain points to target and align product requirements accordingly
- **Delivers technical info on new and updated products to product marketing**
- Works closest with product development and product marketing

- Pricing
- **Market research**
- Go-to-market strategy
- **Product packaging**
- Both influence product development from an end-user and overall market perspective

There are definitely no blurred lines between the two roles at WeTransfer, as Global Product Marketing Manager Melanie Linehan explains:

There's definitely an overlap of where we work together, but I would say that the lines are pretty clearly divided in the sense of, you know, the two of us will work together to understand what the proper message is for what this value of a new feature or product is going to deliver to our users and understanding our users. But our product managers are solely focused on understanding the direction of the product and building out the roadmap. I, of course, will work closely with our product managers to make sure we're prioritizing what marketing needs if there's something within that roadmap that will optimize or help to enable marketing, whether it's monetization of a product or optimization based on an experiment. And then of course my side is to then help make sure that consistency of messaging and the value proposition is constantly and consistently communicated properly across the product. So working with our product designers, copywriters, and then also the marketing team, and with experiments, to ensure that we're always optimizing that as well. So I would say there's overlap, but it's clearly divided as well.

Have you ever asked yourself, "Where you think the line of product marketing and product management should begin and end?" If you haven't, spend a couple of minutes thinking about it now.

_____

_____

_____

_____

_____

Jessica Wright worked with about thirty product managers on forty products at MINDBODY, and she relied on structure to help manage the relationship between product marketing and product management. She says:

We are really disciplined on where we're working and focusing our time. We make sure that we're focusing our efforts on the initiatives that need the most attention and have the most impact. So when it comes to working with product, marketing, and sales, we assess what is being developed that has a large impact on our customers, our market, and the business. We actually developed a system to score our launches, so that takes into account a bunch of variables. Things like impact on revenue, sales effort, whether it's white space or Greenfield expansion, competition, etc., are considered, and then we give every launch a score. What that score does is it puts that launch in a sort of a T-shirt size that then provides a playbook for all the tactics, artifacts, and ceremonies that are typical for that size of product launch. It helps create a common language, ensure you're working on the right things, and that those things can be adequately resourced.

The launch score system Jessica uses was developed internally at MINDBODY, but many product marketers use their own launch tiers to determine how hard to go with their marketing for different launches. You can find ours on the following page.

Prior to the launch score system, Jessica and her team found that despite working closely with product owners, there was always something missed when it came to communicating internally or managing expectations. She says, "We wanted to create this process between product management and product

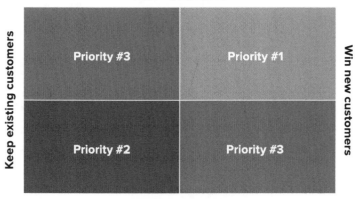

| | Priority #1 | Priority #2 | Priority #3 |
|---|---|---|---|
| In-app message | ☑ | ☑ | ☑ |
| Update existing web pages | ☑ | ☑ | ☑ |
| Add new web pages | ☑ | ☑ | ☑ |
| Positioning/messaging | ☑ | ☑ | ☐ |
| Demo video | ☑ | ☑ | ☐ |
| Social campaign | ☑ | ☑ | ☐ |
| PP PPC campaign | ☑ | ☑ | ☐ |
| Partner campaign | ☑ | ☑ | ☐ |
| Internal training | ☑ | ☑ | ☐ |
| Blog posts | ☑ | ☑ | ☐ |
| Case studies | ☑ | ☑ | ☐ |
| Customer campaign | ☑ | ☑ | ☐ |
| Press release | ☑ | ☐ | ☐ |
| Launch event | ☑ | ☐ | ☐ |
| Webinar | ☑ | ☐ | ☐ |
| White paper | ☑ | ☐ | ☐ |
| Sales battlecard | ☑ | ☐ | ☐ |
| Competitor comparison | ☑ | ☐ | ☐ |

marketing to make sure that everything is covered when we have a product launch. It really helps us with preparing downstream, too, as we can better understand and communicate what type of resources or level of effort is needed for a particular launch. It's a collaborative effort and definitely requires a cross-company input."

It's really important you don't step on anyone's toes in product management, especially in the first few weeks and months. You need to build that relationship, friendship, and mutual trust. It can be so hard to repair the relationship later if you move too fast and don't consider product management's viewpoint.

If you are the first product marketer within a company, you need to take baby steps. The product management team has probably been in place for a number of years, and they will have their share of product marketing. They might even think they should continue to own it. That being said, some product management teams might prefer to "rip the Band-Aid off" and remove themselves from anything that falls within your remit as soon as possible. You won't know which scenario you are facing until you have your initial meetings with the team.

How the product manager/team feels will often come down to their personality type. Without a product marketer, it would have been them having to cover the whole gamut of different relationships—working with everyone from engineering to sales themselves. If they come from a marketing background, it might have been something they felt capable of doing and enjoyed...or it might not.

A big bugbear that PMMs have is that product management doesn't bring product marketing into their plans early enough. They find it frustrating because the product team will wait until they've built a product before they throw it over the fence and say something like, "You go market that now." This is far from ideal and reduces the chances of a successful launch.

In getting your relationship with product management solidified early on, you can be confident that your company's product management person/team understands what product marketing does and how it can help them. This will inevitably lead to them bringing you into this kind of process early moving forward.

We asked Madelyn Wing, Director of Product and Customer Marketing at CallRail, how she proved product marketing's value to the product team:

> When a product manager comes to me and says, "We need to launch this new feature," rather than getting into specifics of dates, where we'll promote, etc. I immediately go for the "why are we building this and who is it for?" I then build out a project plan with the PM, but I show them the upstream work that has to be done before we get into the tactical piece—the messaging, personas, data points that prove our market problem. Over time, by repeatedly

exposing the product team to this upstream work, I've made it clear that this work needs to happen with every single launch and laid the groundwork for the real value a PMM adds. Doing the valuable work to set a strategy in private only keeps the confusing cloud around what product marketers really do—exposing everything that goes into a GTM plan, and how you made the decisions on tactical outputs, is how you really prove your worth.

# CHAPTER 6

# PERFECTING YOUR POSITIONING

To own your internal positioning, you need to truly understand the value you can bring to each team and promote this as much as you can, in the right way.

In this section of the book, we will:

- Explore how different departments can benefit from product marketing.
- Illustrate how crucial segmenting is to show your value.
- Discuss how to sell yourself.

## ILLUSTRATE YOUR VALUE

A value proposition in the context of positioning is basically like a one- or two-liner that companies will use—what it says on the tin—to define their value. And the aim of a value proposition is that your customer or prospect will read it, and then they will just kind of get it. They'll get what you do. They'll get why they need that product, and they'll understand how it's going to benefit them.

So, similarly, you need to do this, but this time, for the customer success teams to instantly understand what product marketing does...then do it for sales, for product, and so on.

You don't want there to be an air of mystery around your role; you've got to break it down for every department. You can't always be saying how they are going to help you; you've got to focus on how you can help them, if you want to get them onboard. Tell them what product marketing means to you, and get an understanding of what they think product marketing is. You can both give your opinion, come together, and then at that point, you can start to formalize your processes. As soon as your understanding is in tune with one another, you can move forward, but it's important to keep having these conversations regularly. If you do, you'll create trust and stay in the loop. If you don't, things could change, and you'll be left out in the cold.

Now you don't necessarily have to do a value-prop piece of work or have an actual value proposition. But you should certainly think about it as it will help you work out your internal positioning and know where to position yourself in meeting with key stakeholders.

**Top tip:** when you are trying to get sales and marketing people bought into new initiatives, it can be a good idea to choose two or three of your sales reps to use as beta testers. You can get them to start using your personas, your positioning, or something else key, then track their calls for a couple of weeks. See if their conversion rate goes up. If it does, you've got the useful data to go into meetings with.

In the meetings, you'll then be able to say something like, "Hey, we've actually been working with these three sales reps, and they've been using the stuff that we provided them, and their sales have gone up by like 5, 6, 7, 8, 9, 10 percent, or whatnot, and they're bringing in however much more revenue." This will give what you say so much more authority as you have data to back up your theories, and the sales reps that took part will feel included and partly responsible for the success. Because you have something tangible to go into meetings, you won't have to deal with sales staff saying, "I don't want to listen to that; I don't want to close more deals."

This way of getting people bought in doesn't work as much with product and customer success teams, so you'll have to show them how you benefit them in a different way.

Making your value proposition known and building trust with different teams is a thankless task. All your processes will need to be continually reviewed and tweaked over time. Some stuff is probably never ending until you get to a certain size, and then that changes. For instance, if you're the first product marketer in your company, your processes will change as your department grows and the different focuses of different marketers come into play.

## SEGMENT YOUR VALUE

As a product marketer, you will work with different teams in different ways, and you'll offer value in different ways too. You need to segment your value by department, as we discussed earlier in Chapter 5 when we looked at creating allies in product management.

Here's what Sebastian Cevallos, Product Marketing Manager at Bell, believes:

> It is so vital, because you need to ensure each team understands the value you bring to the organization, not only so that they benefit from your support, but also so that you are included from the beginning in important conversations.

> Product marketing is a very cross-functional role. We are constantly working with people from different departments, from the product development stage, to a product launch, and more. If other teams, and even the team you report to (Marketing, Product, etc.), are not aware or don't really understand the value we bring and the things we look after/ our responsibilities, we would all see the consequences.

From your initial meetings and research conversations, you will have found out what each department's objectives are, and this will be instrumental in helping you position yourself. Use this information as the backbone of *your* positioning exercise, and feed your role, responsibilities, and expertise into these objectives. The same way tailoring your product's value proposition to different segments of your market will impact how many prospects/customers engage with your product, tailoring what product marketing does to each internal department's specific needs will dramatically increase the attention you attract and buy-in you receive.

If you have been at your company for a while and people still don't value what product marketing does or understand your role, start small and try making it as simple as possible for them. Perhaps don't go all in straight away with the full gamut of your role. Instead, pick the one thing within product marketing that will make the biggest difference to them and start really executing on that to demonstrate value. It could be something like competitive positioning if this is a high priority to your company. Then, over time, start gradually introducing new and impactful elements of your role.

When it comes to how you deliver value to the various departments in your business, there isn't necessarily a one-size-fits-all response. As we've mentioned throughout this book, the stage of growth your ccompany's at, the type of industry it's in, the kind of culture you have, and more, will all influence how you work.

To give you a hand, though, here are some staple sentences that sum up how product marketing benefits and adds value to other teams. Take these and tweak them as you see fit.

**Product marketers help sales teams close more deals by:**

- Equipping reps with sales collateral (like battlecards, product sheets, and sales scripts) so they're able to deliver stronger pitches with shorter sales cycles.
- Helping them personalize their pitches to various personas, segments, and markets so every sales conversation is relevant.
- Providing key learnings and feedback to help make all sales reps top performers.
- Optimizing the buying funnel and providing more high-quality leads.
- Ensuring reps aren't over- or under-selling your products.
- Delivering product training—including the product's specifications, positioning, pricing, benefits, etc. so each and every rep can talk about their products with confidence.

**Product marketers help product teams deliver better products by:**

- Fueling them with real prospect and customer insights so they know what people do and don't like, what there's demand for, how users are using the product, and more.
- Ensuring all releases are tied to organizational goals.

- Fine-tuning existing products based on customer feedback to ensure ongoing usage and revenue.
- Helping to build out product roadmaps and bringing fresh ideas to the table.
- Ensuring other internal business areas are positioning products correctly.

**Product marketers help customer success deliver better experiences by:**

- Providing in-depth data on things like a customer's goals, pain points, drivers, traits, and so on so they can engage in tailored conversations.
- Setting customers up for success from the get-go and using customer intel to proactively engineer customer satisfaction.
- Equipping customer success with the collateral and training needed to up- or cross-sell products.
- Providing customer-driven feedback on how their processes can be improved.

**Product marketers help marketing bring in more leads by:**

- Arming them with key market, persona, and segmentation data so they can deliver highly targeted campaigns that convert.
- Providing mission-critical positioning, messaging, and storytelling information to improve the impact of campaigns—email, PPC, social, PR, or otherwise.

- Supplying customer case studies for use across the board to add credibility to any campaign.
- Providing customer-driven feedback on how their marketing activity can be improved.

**Product marketers help engineering by:**

- Gathering and sharing good and constructive customer feedback to help develop even better products.
- Helping prioritize (in conjunction with the product team) which features/products should be focused on and when.
- Sharing positive testimonials! Often, engineering can get cut out of those feedback loops. Letting them know how customers are reacting to all their hard work is a great way to build relationships and give well-earned pats on the back.

**Product marketers help executive management by:**

Being the linchpin to growth. A PMM's closeness to the customer, competition, market, and product puts them in prime position to unlock new market opportunities, identify high-performing segments, and set every single internal team up with the tools, knowledge, and know-how needed to convert prospects and/or retain customers. And that's every exec's end goal.

**And finally, product marketers contribute to the business's bottom line by:**

- Being the voice of the customer. This ensures every output is in line with what customers want—happy customers stay longer and buy more, and that increases their CLTV.
- Driving adoption, which leads to loyalty. Loyalty leads to referrals, and referrals lead to sales.
- Helping sales reps increase their win rates. More confident sales reps, shorter sales cycles, and better sales-qualified leads mean reps can spend more time selling and less time convincing.
- Driving data-driven product and feature decisions mean money isn't wasted on unsuccessful releases.
- Having better optimized marketing campaigns equal more deals closed.
- Getting prospects to understand the true value of your product means they're willing to pay more for it—and that's a direct result of product marketing's positioning work and will lead to an uplift in deal sizes.

Never presume each department knows you can help with these aspects—tell them in meetings, emails, presentations, etc.

Sometimes, it can be difficult to articulate exactly what you do for each department, so spend a bit of time thinking about how you work with each of your core internal counterparts and how that subsequently helps them hit their targets.

## SALES

How I currently collaborate with sales:

_____

_____

_____

_____

_____

How this helps sales reps hit their objectives:

_____

_____

_____

_____

_____

## PRODUCT

How I currently collaborate with product:

_____

_____

_____

_____

_____

How this helps PMs hit their objectives:

_____

_____

_____

_____

_____

## CUSTOMER SUCCESS

How I currently collaborate with customer success:

_____

_____

_____

_____

How this helps customer success hit their objectives:

_____

_____

_____

_____

## ENGINEERING

How I currently collaborate with engineering:

_____

_____

_____

_____

_____

How this helps engineering hit their objectives:

_____

_____

_____

_____

_____

## MARKETING

How I currently collaborate with marketing:

_____

_____

_____

_____

_____

How this helps marketing hit their objectives:

_____

_____

_____

_____

_____

## EXECUTIVE MANAGEMENT

How I currently collaborate with executive management:

_____

_____

_____

_____

How this helps executive management hit their objectives:

_____

_____

_____

_____

And now go input this information into your own customized "What is product marketing?" deck.

## HOW DRIFT SOLD PRODUCT MARKETING
## TO PRODUCT AND SALES

Tricia Gellman is the current Chief Marketing Officer at Drift and former CMO of both Checkr and Salesforce Canada. We spoke to her about how she sells product marketing to other teams in the company. Starting the product marketing and product management relationship, Tricia said:

> I think there are multiple things you can do here. The first is explaining to them how product marketing should work with product in a more robust way than just writing the messaging when it's done. And that's been interesting because in a way, it changes the way it creates a true life cycle in the product development, where in order for product to collaborate with product marketing, you have to agree when we're doing research to figure out what we want to go and build. Who are the people we're talking to in the market that are going to figure out what we're going to build? How are we going to prioritize across all the things we could do? And then how are we going to do a formal beta? And what does each group do within that? And then obviously product marketing owning the launch.

> This has been impactful for Drift, because in the past, the process was a little bit more ad hoc, depending on which product team and which product management leaders were doing things. By forcing this idea that there is a sort

of end-to-end role on the product for product and product marketing, the co-founders have started to realize there's a lot more benefit and impact we can have in the market when we think further out. And when we really work together to identify not just the things we're seeing like the bug list and things that are coming from the bottom, but also strategically from the top.

So that's been really good. And at first, they didn't understand that at all, but going through the process and pointing out what we need to do a great launch, we started with the end in mind and then said, "Hey, this launch probably isn't going to be that impactful because we don't have analyst endorsements. We don't have customer quotes. How is the media going to write about this? There's no meat to what we're doing, but then you can't have those things if the product is done. And then a week later, you want to launch it. You know, there isn't enough foresight into what's happening." And so the co-founders started to see that they had done that in the early days, but they had gotten away from it when they started to delegate work down in the organization.

Switching now to the product marketing and sales relationship, as Drift moved upmarket into the enterprise space, Tricia said they very clearly saw they needed to talk to more buyers and that the sales cycle was more complex, which would obviously have a knock-on effect to how the sellers sell.

Here's how Tricia and the team combated this, while simultaneously demonstrating the value of the product marketing function: "If the sales team didn't understand the buyers—because we're not selling to sales; we're selling to marketers—there was a need to kind of fill that gap of who is this person? What do they care about? How do we message them? Versus just, "Hey, I have a feature for you," which maybe was what was happening when we were selling to smaller businesses that could kind of just see the demo and say, "Oh, I see how I'm going to use that. That's great." And we started doing persona research and sharing insight with the entire company on who are these buyers? How do they work together? In doing that and bringing that data to the forefront and bringing those customer interviews through video to the forefront, people started to see the value of that as well. So we've kind of been taking the pieces and doing a part of it, and then saying, by the way, look, we need to implement this into part of our process, and let's now mature our sales enablement process."

## HOW SURVEYMONKEY SOLD PRODUCT MARKETING TO PRODUCT AND ENGINEERING

For Eli Schwartz, Growth Consultant and Advisor and former Director of Growth at SurveyMonkey, the secret was appealing to people's human nature. Eli was the first marketer at SurveyMonkey responsible for anything related to international, and his challenge was getting engineering and product teams that were hyperfocused on US-only growth to start caring about allocating bandwidth for international, even though the revenue was only a fraction of the US growth. Eli found it hard to begin a conversation about potential growth in Germany when the entire German user base was less than the user base in a state like New York.

What he discovered, though, was that using the appeal of numbers, i.e., "We need your help to grow Germany by 10 percent," was never going to cut it. Eli needed to draw attention to his case by appealing to the human motivations of his counterparts, and he discovered an argument like this was much more powerful: "The CEO is very interested in our growth in Germany—yes, I know it's small. Would you be interested in joining that cause? We will have a chance to present our work to the CEO at the end of the quarter."

To keep the team he had gathered motivated, Eli made sure to always share the names of people participating in these efforts in company-wide emails—after all, everyone always likes a little vanity. As a result of all this, ultimately, Eli was successful in getting the resources typically allocated to large global initiatives to help him in his mission of growing only small countries.

# CHAPTER 7

# BE A CLUED-UP COMMUNICATOR

Product marketing is an extremely cross-functional role, and it can be really hard to get into unless you're a strong communicator.

In this section of the book, we will:

- Understand the need to back up your assumptions with data.
- Discuss how to deal with difficult questions or requests.
- Share tips to make you a better communicator.
- Look at other top-rated communication skills you need to master.

Communication might be a soft skill, but we cannot stress how essential it is. Ask any product marketer what the most important skills are, and it's highly likely communication will be in their top two, regardless of their company or status.

Before we dive into this chapter, here's an excerpt from a conversation we had with Meg Scheding, Operator and Strategist, around what the best way to communicate with internal teams is.

You should talk to your internal "customers" the same way that you're talking to your customers. Most people don't want to read, so everything you do should be pretty visual or in a bite-sized format. If you're a good product marketer, you'll know that already. You'll know how to communicate to different segments.

Make sure that when you're trying to show people internally how you're adding value that you consider them a customer. Tie everything to your bottom line; show the sales team an example of a case study, for instance, an example of another salesperson...people are very competitive. You can say, "Why was Ginny top salesperson of the month? Here's one of the reasons why, and we worked on this together and we came up with this sales-specific collateral test that we did with a segment of clients, and here's how it performed." Being able to do that and ensure it's not hard for people to see and understand what the value is, is really important. If they have to read through eighteen bullet points, you're not giving them the information that they need. Then, you want to get those messages to your customers—to your C-suite, to your sales teams, to customer success.

So, it's getting featured in their monthly newsletter, or if they have a weekly meeting where they have to give wins and losses, say it would be really nice to be involved. Figure out what their medium is and then conform to that. Part of being a product marketer is being very humble, and that's not saying that everyone should be able to see a two-page document, single spaced, 11-point font because I can read that.

Ask yourself, how do my internal customers ingest and interpret information? Everyone is going to do that in a different way. And the biggest thing is for you to be able to give them a takeaway at the end, so even if it's just a Slack update where you're like, "Hey, I just made this thing," being able to follow up with something, such as some printed collateral that you can put on someone's desk, is important. When things get lost, that kind of thing ends up on someone's bulletin board or on their queue, right? Because nothing's printed out these days, so you can actually engineer that and make sure it's actually read.

Throughout the rest of this chapter, we'll look at some key aspects of communication and how you can boost your communication skills. Even if you view yourself as a confident communicator, there will still be areas you can improve in.

## KNOW THE IMPORTANT NUMBERS

Whenever you go into a meeting with the CMO, CPO, CSO, CRO, CEO, or other, you must make sure you can quantitatively represent what you're doing. If you get asked a question and aren't sure of the answer, don't be afraid to admit it. Ask if you can go away and find out the information required. If you don't—and you try to dodge the question or give false information—there is a high chance you'll get caught out, and those in the meeting will question whether you are trustworthy.

## DON'T BE AFRAID TO SAY NO

It's easy to say yes to everything, but if you do, you won't be able to actually achieve anything because you're going to burn out. You need to be realistic and not over-promise on what you can deliver to the different teams. Otherwise, you won't do what they've asked, and you'll lose their respect.

Your ability to prioritize needs to be grounded in the company's strategic objectives. So, if you're not prioritizing the strategic objectives, then you're almost by default saying yes to everything.

There are numerous scenarios that can result in you needing to say no, but a fairly common one that most product marketers can probably relate to is around product launches. Understandably, after a PM and engineer have been grafting away on a new feature or product for weeks, months, or even years, they're going to want an all-bells-and-whistles launch for everything they ship, but as you know, you have to be careful about not over-messaging customers and drowning out bigger launches with too many updates. To mitigate this happening on a regular basis and potentially straining precious relation-ships, it can be useful to put a launch tier system in place (we've reshared ours on the following page) so everyone knows what level of attention each release will get from the outset. Hopefully, this will remove the need to say no, period.

Jasmine Jaume, Director, PMM (Support and Platform) at Intercom, added:

> Over time, we've gotten better at prioritizing launches based on a feature's potential impact, but it's still a chal-lenge to get that alignment. Sometimes there are other fac-tors that tie into why people might want a bigger launch, even if it's for internal reasons like morale, so it's a tricky balance. I think on a personal level, I find it hard to say no to helping out or just getting stuck into things even when it's technically not my role. I value being a helpful and collaborative teammate to the people I work with, but I've had to learn how to say no to things when I'm busy, and it was an additional ask.

Saying no to something can be especially hard when you are new to a company. You want to build good relationships and get off on the right foot, but you need to get the balance right. You can be helpful but don't want to take on too many additional things. You also need to build a day-to-day structure that works for you—which can be daunting if you are a new PMM.

| | Priority #1 | Priority #2 | Priority #3 |
|---|:---:|:---:|:---:|
| In-app message | ☑ | ☑ | ☑ |
| Update existing web pages | ☑ | ☑ | ☑ |
| Add new web pages | ☑ | ☑ | ☑ |
| Positioning/messaging | ☑ | ☑ | ☐ |
| Demo video | ☑ | ☑ | ☐ |
| Social campaign | ☑ | ☑ | ☐ |
| PP PPC campaign | ☑ | ☑ | ☐ |
| Partner campaign | ☑ | ☑ | ☐ |
| Internal training | ☑ | ☑ | ☐ |
| Blog posts | ☑ | ☑ | ☐ |
| Case studies | ☑ | ☑ | ☐ |
| Customer campaign | ☑ | ☑ | ☐ |
| Press release | ☑ | ☐ | ☐ |
| Launch event | ☑ | ☐ | ☐ |
| Webinar | ☑ | ☐ | ☐ |
| White paper | ☑ | ☐ | ☐ |
| Sales battlecard | ☑ | ☐ | ☐ |
| Competitor comparison | ☑ | ☐ | ☐ |

Sarah Din, VP of Product Marketing at Unbabel, has some great advice on this:

> Don't wait for the structure to happen; create your own. There is so much variability in the role; my day-to-day focus can drastically shift based on business needs. But over time, I've learned to see trends and patterns. I usually block off certain days for all of my one-on-ones to be more present for my team, without too many distractions. I also block off chunks of focus time on my calendar for "reading, thinking, and doing actual work," because if you don't do that proactively, it's easy to get lost in what everyone else is asking of you. You also have to learn to say no to a lot of things. It's hard sometimes, especially when you're new and trying to prove yourself. Whenever I hire someone new, my first piece of advice is that this is the best time you're going to have here; take the first thirty days to meet new people, build relationships, and do a lot of the learning. And protect your time; be proactive and create that structure in the beginning so you can get into the right working habits with others while setting the right expectations.

She adds, "On the days I get into the zone, I turn off my email and my Slack because notifications of any sort can be so disruptive. I put on my headphones, shut everything off, and just focus—those are my most productive days."

And Jeff Vocell, Director of Product Marketing at Iterable, agrees. He says if you are the type of person or individual that says yes to a lot of various things, then your to-do list can grow quite rapidly and quite significantly, and that's a challenge to deliver on in addition to all the strategic acts of your role. In the context of bringing a product to market, let's say you're collaborating with customer marketing on communicating the new release to existing customers. From customer marketing's angle, they might think, well, it's easier for product marketing to just write the email—they know what the feature is, why it's important, and how we're positioning that feature in the market comparatively to competitors, but also as a broader set of our entire platform.

The challenge here, Jeff says, is that if you're not able to say no, you'll also get similar requests from various other teams, like your new business, SEO, and sales enablement teams. They'll ask you to write content too. You'll get all of these requests to create content *for* people and you'll get mired down, so to speak, and you won't be able to focus on pushing the broader launch or broader product forward because you're so focused on the individual tactical pieces of content that you've now said yes to.

To get away from this, you need to enable other departments to do these tactical pieces self-sufficiently. Say to them, for example, "Hey, here's a positioning document, and with that you can draft the content. I'm happy to be in the review cycle for that content, but I can't necessarily write it for you."

This helps everyone in the broader company and, in reality, is the only scalable way to do it.

Before we move on to other essential product marketing skills, we have one last tidbit of advice on saying no. When turning people down, it can be useful to explain the why behind your no. For example: "Sorry, I can't do this right now because X, Y, and Z are my priorities, and these are essential for [insert project] to go ahead." This all-important context can go a long way in showing you're not saying no to be awkward, but it's because you have a backlog of high-ticket items that take precedence.

## SKILLS PMMS CAN'T SURVIVE WITHOUT

### ABILITY TO LEAD SMALL-GROUP MEETINGS

How people perceive you matters, and being a good leader gives you an aura of authority. Kerensa Hogan, Director of Product Marketing at RingCentral (formerly at Amazon and Twitter), is a huge believer that to be successful, PMMs need to be excellent at small-group communication. She recognizes PMMs rarely ever speak to an audience greater than maybe six people in a room, and a lot of the things we do involve communicating in a small group.

More often than not, PMMs are hosting those conversations because they're trying to keep people informed, gain feedback, establish alignment, or solve problems. Generally speaking, product marketers are often the drivers of the entire workflow.

As such, the ability to understand the dynamics of small-group communication and how to manage the conversation in a small group is so important.

It's also really important to be able to lead those conversations with confidence and give clear direction (a) as to the structure of the meeting, and (b) for what you want people to go away and do *after* the meeting. Delivering great agendas to a group is a surprisingly rare skill, so mastering the basics is a quick and easy way to help yourself stand out from the crowd. Talk articulately, get to the point quickly, make sure everyone understands the value of what you're working towards, get everyone excited, and set super clear action points, assignees, and deadlines at the end.

### LOOK OUT FOR TRENDS

When you're getting customer feedback, it shouldn't be the case that one customer requests something, so you now must go build it. As a product marketer, you need to wait for trends to emerge, and if a lot of customers start saying the same thing, then you might act on it. It's the same for internal requests—if one sales rep comes and says, "Oh, I really need this one-pager on this," okay, well, it's one person asking, but if several people in the organization or several sales reps ask for it, then obviously there's a need.

This will help your internal positioning because it'll show you're not a pushover; you know what you're doing. It will enable you to spend time on the highest-value projects that allow you to deliver real value.

## SEGMENT YOUR MEETINGS

When you organize meetings by department, just tell people what they need to know. You don't want to have a two-hour-long meeting and then for an hour and fifty minutes, it's not relevant to half the people there, then give them a ten-minute slot...it will infuriate people. Have shorter, relevant meetings that have a clear agenda, and always come prepared. Before you book any meeting, ask yourself: Is it needed? Are there better ways to do this?

Always use data and customer insights to back yourself up in meetings, for credibility. If, for instance, you're sitting down with the CEO or the CMO and you're saying, "I want to do this because X, Y, and Z," you will look less credible than if you said, "I want to do this because 60 percent of our customers have said they want X, Y, or Z." It is all about positioning—the why behind what you're doing. You're not just sticking your finger up in the air and saying, "I feel this is a good idea."

Of course, there'll be times where you need to get multiple teams in a room at once and that's fine, but when you can, try to divide your meetings by team and topic so you can keep them all uber relevant and short.

Don't stop your segmentation there though, and if you're building an internal roadmap, consider splitting them up too. This will prevent you from running the risk of diluting each team's tasks and responsibilities and people not paying attention to what they should be focusing on. If sales doesn't need to know about a software migration IT will be doing in week five, don't bother them with it—and vice versa. The simpler and easier you make everything to digest, take away, and act on, the more likely you are to get the results you're after.

All of the above will position you as someone who knows their stuff, doesn't waste their time, gets to the point, and delivers only uber valuable info. This will be great for your reputation and should make others more likely to invite you into their key meetings in return.

**Top tip:** bear in mind not everyone likes sharing their thoughts in front of a room of people. To make sure these people and you don't miss out, create a forum for them to provide feedback more anonymously—either by email or through a survey.

## TAKE OWNERSHIP

There's not much you will do as a product marketer that won't rely on at least one other person or department within the company to get that job done, but you must make sure you don't fall into the trap of always saying, "Oh, yeah, we did this. We did that." It's important for PMMs to still own things and not be afraid to say, "I did this, or the product marketing team did that," because otherwise you run the risk of other departments jumping too much onto it. You might rely on other departments, but it's product marketing that's owning it and leading it.

Some people are under the misconception that in saying "we" a lot, they're building trust, but it can damage the relationship they have with other departments if they're constantly saying that they need that support from other people. Their coworkers could start to think that product marketing isn't really needed; they could just go direct instead.

If you or your team has accomplished something, don't be afraid of taking credit. Each time you do, this will help raise the value of your role.

## ESTABLISH A STRONG TWO-WAY COMMUNICATION CADENCE

If you approach your communication with other teams with empathy, you're almost always going to reach a better outcome and stronger relationship. To be successful, you'll need your customer success and sales teams to share their knowledge of what customers want, what they're complaining about, what they need, etc. The easier you make it for these teams to communicate with you, the more likely they are to do it. If you haven't done it already, you might want to set up Slack channels (or something similar) with your sales team so they can just drop feedback when it works for them, or perhaps something as simple as an Excel sheet where people can drop in bits of ad hoc feedback.

How this is achieved will depend on the company, the culture, whether they're remote or in the same headquarters as you, etc. But the earlier you put processes in place, the easier it will be to maintain. Ask for other teams' input and see how they would like to share the information with you. Try and make it as easy as possible.

If there isn't already a strong and effective platform in place, look into and introduce a communication tool that makes collaboration really easy for everyone—whether they're in the same building or working remotely in a different time zone. The easier you make communication, the more likely everyone is to be forthcoming with it. There are tons of options out there for this, and the one you go for will totally depend on your organization, but apps like Slack, Trello, Asana, and Basecamp, for example, are pretty popular and really easy to use.

Sticking with the theme of making it easy, keep this in mind for things like meeting times and takeaways. For example, if you want a meeting with sales about an upcoming launch, don't put it smack bang in the middle of their morning when they're right in their flow; consider putting it in the calendar for first thing in the morning, or straight after lunch. The attendance rate will shoot up, and you'll also hold their attention much better. Keep the contents of your communication simple too. Just because you understand what ARR and CTLV mean, it doesn't mean your audience does, and just because you need to see all fifty-seven lines of a certain spreadsheet, it doesn't mean they do. The more straightforward you keep things, the more people will engage, understand, and remember what you're telling them.

All of this helps you make the point you need to make to them easier, quicker, and clearer, and they're three components that will certainly help build your internal credibility.

### KEEP TOUCHING BASE

By default, some projects and releases will take longer than others. Sometimes, it might take three months to get a launch out of the door; other times, it might take two weeks. Either way, make sure you and your team take ownership of keeping people in the loop and on track. If there's a change or delay to your schedule, promptly let them know about it and how it affects their involvement.

Also, avoid being loose with what you're after and when you need it. If you need a task completed by January 10, put that deadline on the individual, and don't give them any room to wiggle out of it on a technicality. Document it, share it, and remind them of it. For long-running projects, to prevent it falling off other people's radar, you could do something as simple as circulating an up-to-date version of each department's roadmap, say, weekly or biweekly. This will take a matter of minutes and should serve as a regular prompt and keep others from forgetting their role.

As well as that, if someone's deadline is looming, don't leave it until the day of to ask for it. If you do and they've not done it, you've literally no chance of sticking to your timings. Instead, set a reminder in your diary to check in a few days before with a friendly nudge like, "Hey, I'm just checking in to see if we're all on track for the delivery of [insert task] by [insert date]? Let me know if you need anything else from me."

Again, it doesn't take long at your end and will hopefully stop things from slipping. All this will help you portray yourself as someone who's hot on the pulse of what they're doing, and by sticking to your own deadlines, you'll be able to boost your credibility and internal positioning.

A good tip here is to make sure you are actually helping them get their job done, not policing them. Even while remaining firm on your deadlines, candor goes a long way. If you're looking for some support with this, Kim Scott has some excellent tips on how to care personally while challenging directly in her book, *Radical Candor*.

## BE PROACTIVE

To be a product marketer, you must be driven and not expect to have your hand held. If you want something, very often you'll be the one who has to go out and find it. There will be times when you'll definitely be out of your comfort zone and feel stressed, but it can be the catalyst for great work.

Few product marketers will have experienced the scenario Strategic Advisor Maya Grossman was faced with when she became Head of Global Product Marketing of Microsoft. She recalls:

On my first day at Microsoft, my manager left for a three-week vacation. My entire onboarding was a short welcome...I had no guidelines, no goals, and no one to tell me what to do. I stared at the walls of the empty office and wondered: what am I going to do now?

I was determined to make an impact during my first thirty days, and nothing (including a missing manager) was going to stop me!

I spent the first week reading company resources to learn about my business unit, the market, and the audience. Next, I set up introduction meetings with every team member. Not just to introduce myself but to complete my research.

After two weeks of learning and collecting feedback:
1. I identified the key marketing challenges for my unit.
2. I reviewed the existing resources and found the biggest gaps.
3. I made a (simple) plan with immediate actions on how to fill the gaps.

I didn't create a yearly strategy, and I didn't solve all of our problems. Instead, I found a quick win, something I could do in a short amount of time to make a difference.

Why? Because it's a great way to build your reputation. Showing initiative puts you in the driver seat of your relationship with your manager. You also surprise people—no one expects a newbie to deliver a win within the first thirty days. It sets you apart.

We also spoke to Collette Johnson, Product Marketing Strategist at Redgate Software, about making an impact—especially when you're new to a company—and owning your internal positioning, and her advice is pretty simple: when you join an organization, switch it on one at a time.

You can't be like a bull in a china shop on day one saying, "I'm going to change this, this, and this." If you do, you'll be doomed for failure. You've got to sit back and absorb the organization for a few weeks to see what's going on; then you can make your move. When you sit back and absorb, you start to see where you can make your quick impacts.

Colette added:

At Redgate Software, where I am now, I've been brought into this new product. So, I came in and listened to what everyone had to say about it. I gathered my needs, the organization's needs, and found out what was going on. And from all of this, I knew that the first thing I had to do was get sales to believe in this product and understand this product. I realized that they didn't understand this product. And I thought that's my quick win. And I think what you have to do as a product marketer is take on one challenge at a time.

Then, over time, what happens is you develop this strength. I think where it's difficult is when product marketers come in and they want to save the world in three months. It doesn't work. Your job is to educate an organization. You're also educating multiple teams that are so diverse that when you're trying to pull them all together, you just can't get them all to come along at the same time.

# CHAPTER 8

# PICK THE RIGHT OKRs

If you want to nail your internal positioning, you must stay away from vanity metrics. You need metrics that matter because if you want people to understand the value you bring to the table, you need to be able to back that value up with tangible results.

Yoni Solomon, CMO at Uptime.com, believes the reason for the perpetual lack of understanding of the product marketing role is because the metrics have always been a bit "hazy" and harder to comprehend than traditional marketing metrics like leads and traffic—you could say it's a natural byproduct of working in an intersectional role rather than a traditional one.

To help people "get it," Yoni asks people three very simple questions.

1. How confident are you that your product team is building products that are aligned to real market needs and pain?

2. How confident are you that your marketing team knows enough about what you do to run effective campaigns?
3. How confident are you that your sales team understands what you sell, how it works, how much it costs, and who to sell it to?

If someone balks at any of those three questions—they probably need product marketing. In Yoni's experience, that's typically when the "aha" moment happens.

So, in this section of the book, we will:

- Learn how to choose the right goals and metrics.
- Find out how to tie them to value-led company objectives.
- Hear from product marketing experts on how they select their goals.
- Explain how having the right OKRs can get you noticed.

For this chapter of the book, Mary Sheehan, Head of Product Marketing at Adobe Ad Cloud and world expert on metrics and all things product launches, kindly agreed to share her knowledge.

## VISUALIZATION

Think about the biggest project or product launch you're working on right now and ask yourself:

1. What are the deliverables?

2. Who are the people that are involved in it?
3. What are you trying to accomplish with the project/ product launch?
4. What metrics have you assigned to it?
5. Do the metrics you've chosen roll up to any higher-level goals for your company?

Very few product marketers can confidently answer all five questions, so don't give yourself a hard time if you can't. Question 5 is particularly difficult, and most product marketers would admit that they aren't sure of the high-level goals of their company and therefore have no clue whether their metrics do roll up or not.

## LESSON 1: DON'T BE DISTRACTED BY AN EXCITING CAMPAIGN

Mary's metric journey began when she was a product marketer at Google and they had a major launch coming out at South by Southwest. She admits, "In hindsight, it was a bit of a product marketer's dream because it combined a really cool campaign element with a ton of products that we were trying to bring to market in a really compelling narrative." Mary explains further:

> The concept of the campaign was that we took some of these really famous ads of yesteryear and brought the creatives and copywriters back to reimagine these campaigns for the digital era. We had to teach them how to use computers, show them what digital media was like.

We nailed it, and everyone involved celebrated throughout the whole South by Southwest. A week later, I was at our all-staff meeting presenting the metrics of our launch. I was talking about all the impressions we got, all the retweets...and then my director stops me in the middle of the presentation and says, "Okay, does this matter?" And it felt like a sucker punch to the gut.

I was so devastated that I pretty much fumbled my way through the rest of the presentation. Afterwards, I realized she was right; the metrics I was reporting on didn't matter to the ultimate goals that we had for the campaign. It might have been a wonderful tool for engagement and awareness, but we didn't really drive new prospects, and we had no way to track if the products that we were featuring actually got more adoption.

## LESSON 2: UNDERSTAND THE IMPORTANCE OF MEASUREMENT

We are living in a measurement economy and society where people want to track everything they do. Exercising without Strava, a Fitbit, or Apple recording what we do is deemed by many to be a waste of energy and time.

"From a product marketing perspective, everything is becoming digital, and everything is becoming trackable," Mary says. "Today, we are considered drivers of the business, so we need metrics. We're no longer just making one-sheets and putting messaging together." She goes on to say, "Real-time data is now influencing everything we do with customer pain points and addressing those matters immediately. We have the data to be able to iterate and optimize on our campaigns, our launches, and our biggest programs, in real time. We have the tools; we just need to be brave and use them."

Take a couple of minutes to think about how influential you feel product marketing is when it comes to influencing the goals and strategy of your company. What score out of ten would you give it?

## LESSON 3: METRICS CAN BE CHALLENGING

It's really difficult to measure everything you do as a PMM. A great deal of the role is strategy and positioning. There are lots of different stakeholders with many different goals, and there are several variables and dependencies. It's so challenging. Deadlines change, customers' behavior changes, and traits change...but that's what makes a PMM role so interesting. We have to be able to manage and change in real time.

Mary believes flexibility is key and that there are five steps to metric success:

- Know your stakeholders and get inside their head. Find out which goals they really care about, but make sure that those align to what they're thinking.

- Choose those top-level goals wisely. Put them through your framework of "Does this actually make sense for our business? Are these motivational things that we can have?"
- Align to the metrics that you yourself can own and drive. So, you have the power.
- Know and explore the right tools and budgets with your counterparts.
- Build a flexible measurement plan, and don't forget to report on it monthly, to come back to it, and to iterate on it if you need it.

## PRODUCT MARKETERS' TOP PRIORITY GOALS AND HOW TO LEVEL UP

The Product Marketing Alliance's State of Product Marketing report revealed that over half of the PMMs who took part (56 percent) have their performance measured against how much revenue they generate. Almost three-quarters of people who said this OKR is used to track their performance worked in B2B, with this OKR not so much a priority for PMMs in B2C companies.

Roughly one in six (14.7 percent) of the product marketers who took part don't have OKRs in place, which could be because the companies they work for don't know how to accurately measure or track their success.

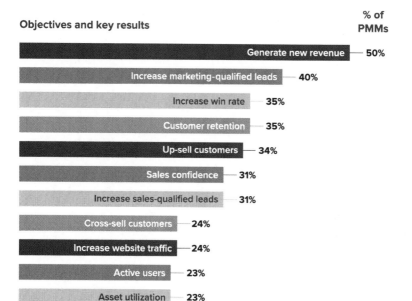

**Objectives and key results**

% of
PMMs

- Generate new revenue — 50%
- Increase marketing-qualified leads — 40%
- Increase win rate — 35%
- Customer retention — 35%
- Up-sell customers — 34%
- Sales confidence — 31%
- Increase sales-qualified leads — 31%
- Cross-sell customers — 24%
- Increase website traffic — 24%
- Active users — 23%
- Asset utilization — 23%
- Customer satisfaction scores — 19%
- Increase trial sign-ups — 18%
- We don't have OKRs — 15%
- Time taken to complete actions — 8%
- Other — 5%

Looking at the top scoring objectives on this report can be a good starting point when trying to come up with your own goals. Three of the most common PMM goals are growing revenue, increasing product usage, and decreasing churn. These are top-level goals that matter and can be measured and benchmarked accurately.

Is customer usage growing?

- **Product usage:** how often are users coming back?
- **Product growth:** how much has product usage increased?
- **Churn:** are new customers staying with us?

How many customers are we acquiring?

- **Leads:** are we on target to hit the quota we've committed to?
- **CAC:** how much does it cost us to get a new customer?
- **LTV:** what is the total value of our customers by segment?

Will we hit revenue goals?

- **Revenue:** will we hit quarterly revenue targets?
- **Time to close:** how can we close deals faster?
- **Pipeline:** are we on track for success?

Here are some of the top metrics that PMMs can own:

- Daily active users (DAUs)
- Monthly active users (MAUs)
- New users
- Feature adoption
- Product adoption
- Content downloads
- Demo requests or views

- Product landing page conversion
- Sales pipeline increase
- Customer win-rate increase
- Product usage tracking
- Time to close
- Win rate
- Average contract value
- Churn rate
- Customer satisfaction

Win rates can be something that PMMs can really influence through positioning, through major product launches, and through programs they're running with prospects. Sales in particular will be interested in whether you are able to track the overall win rate compared to all the pitches that are happening with customers, but you may find that this is of interest to everyone.

There are two ways that win rates can be calculated:

1. Accounts won over the total pitches out there
2. The amount of revenue won over the total potential revenue out there

You may want to track both ways as this will allow you to ask this question: "Are some of our competitors taking a bigger share?"

With launches, PMMs can influence increasing product usage. You can track new feature adoption, the number of active users, and decreasing churn. You can see whether your existing customers are sharing your blogs, watching your videos, and downloading your white papers.

Pendo and Amplitude are great tools for tracking product usage. Some products for tracking content usage can be expensive, but they are well worth it for what they give you. Mary warns:

> If you are putting content out there and you're not tracking it, goodbye, your one-sheet is going into the great abyss and you'll never have any feedback. You'll beg the sales team to tell you, Oh, are you using this deck? Are you using this one-sheet? You might get a couple of comments. But honestly, it's on to the next thing after that content is out there. So if you can have a content management platform that helps you track things like views, downloads, and shares, that really is an indicator of decreasing churn as well as new revenue growth.

To quantify stakeholder satisfaction as much as possible, consider having pre and post surveys before you launch a new set of materials or a new positioning. This will allow you to see what their perception of the PMM team is. If they don't feel that they're getting the materials they need to do their jobs effectively or lack opportunities to give you feedback, you can put this right. Finding out what your stakeholders think of you can really help you grow and develop—remember to ask for this information anonymously though; you want—and need—candid feedback.

Once you've considered all this, you can build your flexible measurement plan:

- Create a baseline. Even though it's scary, you've got to start somewhere. How are we going to get those metrics that we wanted to track?

- Figure out a way to report on it. Have someone on your team manage it monthly. You should pull the metrics monthly, but just have something that you come back to. Don't set it and forget it. This is something you should be owning and working through.

- Iterate. If there's a metric that's not working for you or something that comes up that you think you should be tracking, we are in the digital age. Don't feel like this is totally set in stone.

To find out more about metrics, why not connect with Mary Sheehan on LinkedIn? Or check out her book, *Product Launch Enablement and Strategy, Explained*.

## PRODUCT MARKETING METRICS IN ACTION

When Tricia Gellman, now CMO at Drift, worked at Adobe, she had a number for the product. When Tricia worked at Salesforce, there was no number, and even though she loved product marketing, not being held accountable for something was a struggle because she wanted to see she was achieving something.

Back then, adding videos to websites was a new thing, and a key focus point for Tricia and the team. They'd have to create concise, clear messaging, positioning demo videos, and then they were measured on whether or not people watched the videos and how far they watched through the videos because if the message was rubbish, people would clearly drop out.

Tricia said:

> It was really a struggle. I think one of the reasons a lot of product marketing lives in product is because it is easier to measure the adoption of a product, and I think that's something product marketers should be measured on. If you're working on a product line, how much is that product being adopted and how deep is that adoption? If you have twenty-five features, is it that two get used or is it that twenty get used and that's kind of more to that first phase of being involved in understanding the customer need and then delivering on it. I think if you're involved in that phase and you do that well, you can measure the fact that customers gave good reviews.

Adoption metrics are, in today's world, pretty normal for people because there's a lot more technology to do that. So, I think that's the easy part. The harder part is on the rest, the messaging for the positioning of the company or the sales enablement. We are currently defining metrics for product marketing, one in terms of share of voice. So, when we launch things and we have good messaging in the market, how much do we kind of continue to lift ourselves in the conversation within our category and within our buying group?

The second thing is on deal size and close-win rate. So, if we enable the sales team with differentiated messaging, they should be able to command a higher value and they should be able to win at a higher rate. And so, we should be able to see that continually rising. And then the third thing I would say is with the go-to-market demand-gen team, you can start to do A/B testing so if you have solid messaging that you're working with them on, you could see the conversion.

## GETTING THE BALANCE RIGHT

There needs to be visibility into what you're doing. If people can see your wins, it will breed future buy-in. Once you have your chosen metrics and you're doing well and you're hitting them, you need to communicate them out if you want to get people to understand the value and benefits of these metrics. It will differ from organization to organization, but it's just as important that you don't *over*communicate as it is that you don't *under*-communicate. There may already be communication processes in place, but if there aren't, you'll need to start from scratch and think about what would be the best way to go about it.

You should also be sharing failures. People may offer support and ideas that result in shared wins and stronger relationships.

When you do communicate, make sure you are talking about the numbers that matter. Otherwise, you'll run the risk of product marketing sending a monthly update when there's not really much in there for people, and they won't open it.

Make it a compelling read too so that people pay attention to your OKRs and the success you have had. Explain how they impact the organization's objectives so people can easily see the bigger picture—but don't hide things that haven't worked; be upfront and honest. It's obviously human. Not everything you do is going to be a great success. At the end of the day, it's about framing the campaigns or OKRs you've set but not achieved in such a way that doesn't lose credibility.

When the numbers aren't great, evaluate why. Admit that, okay, we didn't hit this campaign; it didn't work because this, this, and this. However, moving forward, you'll do this, this, and this. This will result in the losses not being just construed as losses. They will help you be even more successful next time—and remember to communicate this kind of evaluation out too.

Don't see missed targets as a failure or reflection on you. It takes a strong leader to own their losses as well as their wins, and owning them in the *right* way can actually add to your credibility.

Collette Johnson, Product Marketing Strategist at Redgate Software, adds:

> If you do a product launch and it fails, you haven't failed. Something's happened; go back, analyze it, critique it, talk about it as an organization, and learn from it. It doesn't matter whether you're in B2B or B2C. B2C definitely sees far more failure, but failure hits everybody all the time; it's just part of the job. Anyone who says they haven't ever failed isn't telling the truth. We've all had them. We all have those stories. Most of us hide those stories.

> People think that the success of their next role lies in the success in their previous role, and I just don't agree with that. If I had been interviewing somebody and I said, "Talk to me about a failure and how you approached it," and they said, "I haven't had one," I'd just think they're not telling me the truth. But if somebody talks to me about that failure and they tell me what they learned, or they've looked at it from an objective viewpoint, that to me is a good marketer because they have looked at it and they've moved on from it, and they've drawn a line under it and they've learned. I know that a marketer who can talk about that will be able to talk about any issues we have in the future.

# Setting Personal Goals

So far in this chapter, we've spoken mainly about product marketing metrics, which, if you are part of a product marketing team, will likely be collective objectives. For both your personal and professional development, it's also a good idea to set some trackable, personal goals—you could set these yourself, or in conjunction with your manager. Individual goals are crucial in enabling you to see the difference you're making individually on a week-by-week basis. Individual goals are also really important in helping you hone your soft skills. For example, just because your product marketing teammate is a great presenter and communicator, it doesn't mean you are, and working on this will help you improve your internal positioning as well as the team's. However, these kinds of personal and professional goals can go neglected unless you are proactive in improving them.

Pick meaningful goals that, when met, have a notable difference on how you perform in your role.

## RECOGNIZE THE DIFFERENCE BETWEEN INTENSIVE AND EXTENSIVE VALUE

Having intensive value is dependent on one key skill that you have developed. You are an expert in a certain aspect of product marketing, so you become the go-to person in that area. Whereas with extensive value, it involves your relationship with lots of different people who have lots of different skills. You are a connector; you make sure that different projects are running to plan, and you resolve issues between different teams. You are a mediator.

As a product marketer, you need to consistently show intensive and extensive value to people within your organization, and you should always be working to improve your knowledge and skills. Building relationships will always be a crucial part of the role.

To improve your intensive value:

- Enroll in courses in your chosen area.
- Read extensively.
- Connect on LinkedIn and/or network with key people in your chosen area.
- Work outside of your day job on projects that will help you gain knowledge in this area.
- Join the PMA's Slack community and other useful communities.
- Join a mentorship program.

To improve your extensive value:

- Find out how different departments are interlinked.
- Find out what projects/products each team is working on, even if they are outside of your remit.
- Chat with people in the cafeteria/elevator, and go for a coffee.
- Be as approachable as possible.
- Help people when you can—inside and outside of work.
- Connect people from different departments.

## OWN YOUR GOALS

Spend a few minutes thinking of three goals you can set for yourself and the best success metrics you can use:

- Goal 1:

  _____

- Intensive or extensive value:

  _____

- Success metrics:

  _____


- Goal 2:

  _____

- Intensive or extensive value:

  _____

- Success metrics:

  _____

- Goal 3:

  _____

- Intensive or extensive value:

  _____

- Success metrics:

  _____

**Top tip:** you should also do your own personal performance review each month. Be tough on yourself, and if you haven't delivered on one of your goals, make sure you put in some extra effort so that you'll achieve it next month. Write up your review and if it feels appropriate, send it on to your manager so you can discuss it in person.

Less is more, so try to limit yourself to no more than three hundred words per review. Keep them all together so you can look back over them before your annual review. This will jog your memory and help you remember all the key achievements you've had over the previous twelve months.

Also, don't wait for feedback; send out a Google Survey each month to hear what others think. Ask if there's anything you're not doing that they think you should, or if there's anything you're currently doing that you should stop working on. Acting on this feedback isn't necessary, but it's always important to consider it.

CHAPTER 9

# FACING RESISTANCE

During your product marketing career, you may work for a company that, despite your best efforts, still doesn't value the role of a PMM. It's important to not let this bad experience leave you feeling deflated and questioning whether you're good at your job.

In this section of the book, we will:

- Discuss how you can win people over.
- Recognize when it's time to let go.
- Think about the lessons we can learn from bad experiences.

## HITTING A BRICK WALL

It's important to be open and talk about negative things.

Collette Johnson has had several bad experiences and is open to sharing them in the hope that it will help other PMMs going through similar experiences. When she joined a data visualization startup, she initially thought that she'd struck gold because the visualizations of mapping data were beautiful. She said:

> You could map global carbon emissions data and you could see where it was at the ports, and it had a beautiful interface so I felt that I could market this to anyone, and anyone could understand it. And I remember going to my first meeting where they referred to me as the head of glitter, and straight away, I thought, Oh, what have I done? I was the first marketer there and all of a sudden, I realized that this company didn't really want marketing.

> Later, when my team moved from sitting in the senior team office to be nearer to product, the COO came over to our bank of desks and said, "All we need now to complete this team is some colouring books and crayons." I remember just being completely horrified at that thought, thinking, actually, you really don't understand what marketing does.

> And that was really difficult for me because I had to try and change the perceptions of people who were very stuck in their ways and make them understand what marketing really was and the value it brought. I remember saying to them, "The first thing we've got to do is go out to

customers, to clients, and understand what people want to do with this product." There was so much resistance, the head of product said he knew how people would use the product, but he hadn't spoken to a single person; he just had this perception. He had just read things on the internet...it just made me realize they didn't value the customer insights.

Thankfully, other people in the company supported me on this and I said, "Well, we're going to do it." So, I arranged to go visit a friend of mine, so I knew that it was an easy visit. I prewarned this friend of mine saying I'm sending some of my company to you, but be warned, they're very resistant and there is a little bit of aggro. They needed to learn and understand that user without me there.

So, I sent them for this day out to watch how people were looking at data, how people in tech are using data. And the product team were basically looking at behavioral insights, how do you look at how customers behave and push advertising at them. And they came back the next day, and they were very quiet, and I thought, nope, nobody's been to see me yet. And I went over to them and said, "How did it go?" "Oh, it's great. And they do this. And they do that." And all of a sudden, I saw what had clicked. They wouldn't admit they were wrong, and I didn't need them to admit that they were wrong, but they understood the user for the first time and realized they had not designed a product for the user.

That was a big pivotal change for me because all of a sudden, the product team started to realize the value I could add into their development. And it was really interesting because then we started to develop this product, we started to get user insights, and it was great.

And then that company took another pivot just as we were getting there with marketing. We'd re-messaged the product, we'd repositioned it, and it was working. The CTO and the CEO started to get more involved in engagements and going out to sales.

We had started to get really good PR and media traction, and we had people coming to us about the product. We thought we'd clinched it. And then we went to this management meeting. And they came in and said, "Oh, we've met this client and we're doing this. We're getting rid of the visualization part of the product." I was like "What? You can't just say that; this is the whole selling point of the product. We've spent months figuring this out. We have got it to work." And they just responded by saying, "Well, we went to a client and they said this, so just get rid of it. We're going to be a database now." I said, "Look at all this evidence; look at what we've done," and I showed them where we'd gotten all the traction, and they just didn't get it.

They didn't validate these users. And I think it's interesting that that company where marketing didn't really work was due to them pivoting the whole product based on one meeting with one client. So, you would never plan for success. As a product marketer, it's all about evidence and clients. This is where the majority of your pot of gold is. You might have this tiny pot here, but it's not going to make you sustainable.

I left that company a handful of months ago because I thought, "They're just not open to this." And I pushed and pushed and pushed and pushed. I turned the product team around. I worked so hard to make that product successful and worked against any people who didn't believe in marketing and thought it was just a tick box. It's so sad because that company has no more funding and has failed. It couldn't secure clients because they took away the one valuable part of that product, which was the visualization.

## SAME SCENARIO, DIFFERENT REACTION

Collette continues:

I've been to other organizations, like Plextek, where they did no marketing whatsoever until I got there, and the reaction was the complete opposite. The CEO, Nick Hill, was a man who just embraced so much change in an organization. I said, "Right, we're going to do marketing and we're going to make it work. We're going to productize. We're going to product market. We're going to position this.

We're going to go market-led." And he said, "Okay. You've got the reins, take it." And I did it, and I just changed that organization.

I met with him about eighteen months ago when I was having to deal with all the negativity of my last company and doubting myself. And he sat with me and he said, "There's one thing you've got to remember that you achieved at Plextek...you gave us marketing and that has changed our business completely. You have to be proud of that because before you came, we never had it. And now we have it, and it is key to everything we do." He totally got it.

**Top tip:** If somebody doesn't want to come along on your product marketing journey and they resist that journey, and you've tried some tactics to turn them around—brought them in, shown them evidence, discussed, tried different ways of moving them—don't keep pushing. It just won't work. There are times you must leave some people behind. And there are people you will never change, people who will never come on that journey with you. And that's fine. That is not a failure on your part.

## TOO LATE TO THE PARTY

Another relatively common area of resistance for product marketers can be the stage in which they're brought into the product roadmap—and this is detrimental to everyone's success.

We mentioned it earlier in the book, but a common notion among some is that "product managers put products on the shelf, and product marketers get products off the shelf." We all know how false that is. Resistance from your product management team here can really stifle not just your success but the success of the product and company too. We won't go into it in too much detail again here (flip back to the "Create allies in product" section in Chapter 5 for more), but breaking down that resistance by clearly communicating your role in the roadmap, how you can add value to the roadmap, and where the lines between product management and product marketing converge and stop will be crucial to smoothing out this barrier.

Have you also experienced a company that was resistant to product marketing and another that fully embraced it? Or maybe you faced negativity from some colleagues in an organization that was pro-product marketing overall?

Think about three lessons you have learned from your experiences, and jot them down here:

Lesson 1:

_____

_____

_____

_____

Lesson 2:

_____

_____

_____

_____

Lesson 3:

_____

_____

_____

_____

If you are currently going through a tough time, don't be afraid to speak out and connect to other PMMs who can support and guide you. The PMA has lots of members who are more than willing to help—Collette included.

Take a few minutes to think about any problems/pain points you have and brainstorm possible solutions that will, in turn, assist you with your internal positioning:

Problem / Pain point 1:

_____

_____

Possible solution/s:

_____

_____

_____

_____

Problem / Pain point 2:

_____

_____

Possible solution/s:

_____

_____

_____

_____

Problem / Pain point 3:

_____

_____

Possible solution/s:

_____

_____

_____

_____

# CHAPTER 10

# HANDS-ON, VALUE-ADDING TIPS

The best advice you can get as a product marketer is from people who have been there and got the T-shirt.

In this section of the book, we will:

- Bombard you with the best tips from the crème de la crème of product marketing.
- Share tips for adding value in meetings, updates, finding the right role, and everything in between.
- Look at some of the most common mistakes (and perhaps some not so common).

# TIPS FOR ADDING VALUE IN MEETINGS

## BE THE LAST ONE TO TALK!

Duong Tran, Marketing Manager at RBC Ventures, strongly believes this:

> I think when you're in a meeting, as a PMM, it's easy to say, "Customer support, do this; sales, do this," because you touch different areas of the business. It's important to absorb all the information first and then formulate your opinion and questions after that.
>
> Once you have the understanding in the whole meeting room, then you can start asking better questions. Otherwise, you can start poking at things that don't make sense in part of the business. So, for example, if I'm in a meeting with different heads of the departments and they're trying to find a solution to one problem, I can't provide a solution if I don't know everything that's happening. I don't have enough knowledge to have an opinion. Let's figure out what the problem is, what areas people can add value, and then you can start asking questions—at the very end, once you understand.

## ILLUSTRATE HOW YOUR WORK FEEDS INTO SALES/CUSTOMER SUCCESS REVENUE

Duong admits:

I'm a visual person, so I think having diagrams or sketches of boxes and arrows and how things connect can really help connect the dots. Metaphorically yes, but also really being visual in showing how your work impacts different parts of the business. I think it's really important to give everyone a full view of what's happening. It doesn't have to be a fancy diagram. It could be as simple as sketches, or rough diagrams, or whatever. Visual pieces help you find the gaps and be more granular about what's happening.

## MAKE IT INTERESTING

In your regular meetings, always come in with an agenda of what you're going to cover. Product Marketing Leader Shirin Shahin says:

A lot of times it really depends on who you're meeting with. If you're meeting with product management, they'll be curious to see what you're working on and want to tell you what they're working on. They'll want you to update them on the go-to-market planning and where you are, it's important for them to see. The product managers are so involved in building the product they don't really get to see what happens after they build the product, so I think that's a really great way to show that view.

And then if you're meeting with sales, the different tools and enablement tools you're working on is really important to show them. Always add value to every meeting by bringing what you're working on that is relevant to that person.

## ALL-ROUND PRODUCT MARKETING TIPS

### BE READY FOR ANYTHING!

When COVID-19 hit the world in spring 2020, Sebastian Cevallos was the Product Marketing Specialist at fitness brand Merrithew. They had to move fast as their studios were closed and everything moved online. They had been planning on launching a new media streaming platform on their website at the end of the year but moved it forward to April. He explains:

> I think this is rare to move such a big launch months ahead, but we made it work; we did a soft launch, which I didn't love the idea of, but we had to, and then we did a proper big launch in May. It was management who decided on the pricing and title of this, and then they announced it to the VP and the marketing team. I had to share with her my competitor research and competitor table, and I was like FYI, there is a direct competitor that uses the exact same video streaming, so the user interface will be exactly the same. They also have the same name. So, I said, "I see an issue with that," and by sharing all the data and knowledge of the competitors and what they were doing, we were able to change the pricing, structure, and the name of the product. It's so important. Imagine any big brand, like if Samsung dropped a brand that sounded like iPhone

or something like SamBook—like MacBook—it wouldn't work. It would be like you're clearly copying one another... so keeping an eye on competitors is something that a product marketer must do.

## BE FLEXIBLE

Dekker Fraser, a Product Marketing Consultant, thinks this is key:

> Years ago, I crafted the "perfect" web page based on detailed data analysis and finely tuned copywriting. Later, I discovered that the product manager had made some major changes to that page that seemed arbitrary rather than grounded in data. This small incident created a lot of unnecessary stress for me but taught me a lesson far more important than the outcome of that page: be flexible. The choice to be flexible and let go of perfectionism has relieved me of so much stress as a PMM. It taught me to get input from other departments early in the process, before I finalize the details, and to not get too personally invested in my projects.

## DON'T HAVE A BIG EGO

Product marketing is almost like a behind-the-scenes ingredient for greatness across all different teams, but sometimes product marketers can have too much of an ego. Tricia Gellman, CMO at Drift, explains:

It can be a detriment because people perceive that you're trying to take what they do away from them. And it creates more of a barrier for them to adopt wanting to work with product marketing. It can lead to the product team thinking, well, we define the product, what are you going to bring to the table? And if you have a big ego and you're like, well, I own this and I'm going to be the one that knows everything...I'm just going to tell you what to do, then nobody will want to work with you. The same applies with sales and the other teams. I think that's the balance with product marketers; product marketers have to kind of absorb the key metrics and the key needs of all these groups. And at the same time, kind of plug in to help them all be better versus trying to come and be the savior and the hero that fixed everything.

## SMALL TWEAKS CAN HAVE A BIG IMPACT

Never underestimate yourself and your ideas. Adam Cason, Vice President, Global and Strategic Alliances at Futurex, shares:

Sometimes making a tiny change to product positioning can have a huge effect. We saw this when we renamed our tiered technical support offerings. We originally used "Standard" and "Platinum," with the significant majority of customers opting for the lower-end option. After we made a simple name change to "Non-Business Critical" and "Business Critical," our premium offering became the de facto standard almost overnight.

## DO YOUR RESEARCH FIRST, AND DON'T BRING OTHERS IN TOO EARLY

Jay Rusden, Strategic Marketing Consultant, thinks that one of the biggest common mistakes that a product marketer can make is doing what he calls "outsourcing your work internally." Here's what he says:

> For example, let's say you're working on a segmentation strategy, pricing offer, or a launch plan—it's very easy to develop those things almost entirely using input from the product team or sales teams, as they have very strong opinions on how they would like to see things happen.

> Whilst it is important that stakeholders provide insight and input on these types of topics, it's fundamental to being a great product marketer that you first do your research and formulate a well-developed strategy based on available data, voice of the customer, and competitive intelligence and only then leverage internal resources for the final adjustments and perspectives needed to get it to the finish line. This will help position you as a far more valuable resource in the business and ensure that your approach is not overly influenced by opinions that are not underpinned by research.

## LEARN TO PRIORITIZE

This is really key, and for most product marketers, it's a work in progress. Medha Pratap is Director of Product Marketing at Syndigo. She says:

My biggest challenge as a product marketer has been prioritization. Championing sales, product, marketing, and customer needs as well as multiple product lines can be challenging at times. Project management skills are essential to product marketing. Staying organized and ensuring that successful launches are carefully planned is crucial. Leading up to a launch, all updates must be reflected, and customer-facing teams should be provided with necessary materials.

Outside of a product launch, a product marketer's priorities can shift hourly. It is really important to assess the difference between "important" and "urgent." I have tried to level up my organizational skills with project management systems and blocking off time to work on tasks. I have also been saying "no" more, which is a personal challenge. But "no" really means "not right now." I clearly articulate where a project fits with other responsibilities at any given time. It is important to set boundaries and tread a fine line between being helpful and not neglecting priorities. While I have made strides in prioritization, there are always untapped opportunities to better align activities with product roadmap and customer needs.

## FIND LEVERAGE IN PARTNERSHIP

Product marketing will never scale as fast as its partner stakeholder teams in product or sales. But, by partnering with other teams like solutions engineering and sales enablement, you're able to find leverage and scale your impact on the organization. Patrick Cuttica, former Director of Product Marketing at Sprout Social and now Senior Product Marketing Manager at Square, said:

> An ethos I've tried to instill with my team from the beginning is, "Do great work, and be great partners to work with." This may sound like a platitude (it sort of is), but it implicitly highlights the cross-functional nature of the product marketer's job. I've been intentional in socializing this ethos across the company through All-Hands meetings, cross-departmental emails/newsletters, etc. to make it incredibly clear that our success as a product marketing team is inextricably linked to the success of the teams with which we partner.

## TIPS FOR FINDING THE RIGHT ROLE

### UNDERSTAND WHAT YOU WANT

Meg Scheding, Operator and Strategist, is a huge advocate of this. She says:

> Spend time thinking about what you really want out of a product marketing position. And what you know of product marketing doesn't have to be a one-size-fits-all for every position. So there's some large entities like an Intuit or an IBM or a Cisco where there are so many products and services; they may have you—as a product marketer—only work on sales enablement. Help the seller sell the product.

And what you'll probably end up doing for a larger company is selling how you can expand the role of product marketing to encompass more things. So, you just have to be a very good translator and promoter of what that company is expecting in terms of product marketing and being able to have that conversation especially when you're job searching and talking to potential employers. What is their definition? A lot of folks when interviewing as prospective employees are asked what is product marketing, but you should be turning that around on the employer and asking them what they think product marketing is. Because then you're able to educate them (and you'll sound very smart) and say there's many tenets to product marketing. You'll also have a much better chance of understanding whether it's the role for you, to be able to have any growth at that organization.

### DON'T BE AFRAID TO EDUCATE

Puja Shah, Product Marketing Manager at LBMX, started her PMM career in India before moving to Canada in 2018. She says:

> When my husband and I decided to move to Canada from India, our research indicated there would be great opportunities for our careers and life in the Toronto and Vancouver regions. Even before we arrived in 2019, my spouse landed a job offer in London, ON and we decided to begin our Canada life in this city although we weren't sure if I would also bag an equally satisfying career opportunity. But we made a joint decision to take this leap of faith.

As we started living here, I was fortunate to be introduced to the city's economic development corporation, and they helped me get face time with CXOs at several IT companies in this city. To be honest, there aren't as many tech firms here compared to some of the bigger cities in Canada; however, the ones which are, are doing very well for themselves in their niche. However, I realized I was spending a lot of time educating these firms. Right from the interview stage, my role would begin as an educator—defining what is PMM, what is the role of a PMM, where does the function fit in the organization, who the PMM reports to, what are the other key product marketing roles, and how do you measure the success of a PMM department.

Not gloating about myself, but most of them were impressed with our discussions. One well-known firm formally rolled out a PMM job opening on their website after receiving my CV. Within a month of meeting C-level executives in the city, I landed my first job as a PMM. I am definitely the first PMM in the two-decades history of my employer and probably also the first PMM in London, ON.

## VARIETY IS THE SPICE OF LIFE

Early on in your career, have a multifaceted approach and try as many different roles as possible. Take a stab at content writing, event marketing, product marketing, or demand generation. Even within product marketing, there are many options. Are you driven by metrics or are you a storyteller? No matter what direction you take, experimenting and putting yourself in every marketer's shoes will help you become a stronger PMM and contribute to the win.

### DO WHAT MAKES YOU HAPPY

This tip is courtesy of Dekker Fraser, Product Marketing Consultant:

> Do what makes you happy and don't be distracted by fancy titles and brand names. I turned down a CMO position to pursue my own projects and turned down other high-title, high-pay jobs for the sake of gaining the right kind of experience. Gain experience doing what you enjoy, and you'll be handsomely rewarded in the long run.

## RELIABILITY, TENACITY, AND OWNERSHIP

For this section of the book, we spoke to Teresa Haun, Director of Product Marketing at Zendesk, about a couple of her top tried and tested career-building tips.

The first is showing consistent reliability and tenacity. Showing you are consistently reliable and tenacious means becoming a person everyone can count on to get the job done and done well. Everyone wants to work with someone like this because they don't have to worry. There is no question you'll successfully complete your responsibilities in a workstream, and if you hit roadblocks, you won't just give up. Instead, you'll find smart ways to unblock the path.

In product marketing, this might mean finding a creative compromise between the needs of product and sales or promoting marketing assets in new ways when the usual channels are full. Showing consistent reliability and tenacity means you'll always be a dependable, cross-functional partner and teammate who produces high-quality work regardless of the challenge.

Teresa reflected:

> I have been fortunate to have a number of memorable moments in my career where I've seen the direct benefits of being reliable and tenacious. The most salient one was actually before I started working in product marketing, during my time working in financial forecasting at Gap Inc. There was a major, new type of forecast needed for one of the largest areas of the business with a very tight timeline. Our brand president was especially concerned and decided to bring together her team of senior leaders to discuss how to ensure this forecast was done well given the impact on this large area of the business. I was not in this meeting, but my boss told me that our brand president continued to reiterate how apprehensive she was, until she heard who was going to be owning the forecast. As soon as my boss said that I was the one who would be responsible for it, our brand president said, "Oh, Teresa is

the one working on it? If that's the case, we're totally fine."
It was an incredibly flattering moment to feel the trust that
our most senior leader had in my work and that she had
no doubt she could count on me to get the job done and
done well.

The second of Teresa's tips is having a bias for action and taking ownership. This trait can be especially impactful in large
cross-functional work streams where there isn't a clear next
step or path forward as well as limited clarity as to who should
own what. It can be challenging in these broader group settings
to make efficient progress as discussing and working on every
single piece together with a large number of people isn't often
effective or realistic. Teresa tends to see progress is made once
someone actually starts taking a stab at next steps and giving the
rest of the group something to discuss and react to rather than
coming up with all that collectively. This often means that as the
initiator, you also become the clear leader in determining the
path forward for the whole team and setting an example for people to start making progress. It's a huge opportunity to shine if
you can have that bias for action and step up to take ownership.

Teresa said:

> An example of where I directly saw the benefit of this prin-
> ciple in my work experience was for a major cross-func-
> tional initiative that was a huge financial opportunity
> for our business and involved almost every team at our

company. We had a working group of fifteen senior leads from across the business and were meeting every couple of days to discuss and try to make progress. Weeks started to go by where we just continued discussing and trying to align on everything as a group, and as a result, we were progressing significantly slower than needed to get this major initiative developed, scoped, and executed in time. This was exactly where having a bias for action and the willingness and desire to lead and take ownership really made a difference. I was able to exhibit this by shifting our frequent group meetings to discuss and react to work that I had already taken a first stab at.

Each meeting, I would show up with the next iteration of a key piece I thought we needed and walk through the rationale for the decisions I had made to then gather the group's feedback and input. In advance of every single meeting, I would make sure I had done more work indi-vidually, incorporating prior feedback and taking a stab at the next piece to then share with the broader group. As a result, I saw our conversation in each meeting become so much more productive, with the focus shifting to discuss that work I had already done in advance each time, rather than just collectively trying to do the work hand-in-hand from scratch during the meeting with a huge group.

I received very positive feedback on my initiative to do this from the team, and many also then seemed inspired to follow suit, finding other parts of the project they could individually tackle first and bring back to the group for feedback. Also, as a result of showing this bias for action and taking ownership, my role in the entire initiative evolved to become one of the clear leaders across the whole working team. I had the opportunity to significantly shape the outcome of the initiative, which had a big financial impact on our entire company.

## WHAT TO DO

No product marketer's ride is completely smooth, and even the biggest names in product marketing have made mistakes during their careers—and they make us stronger and better. Here are a few bloopers kindly donated from our awesome community of PMMs.

### MAKE SURE YOU CONSIDER CUSTOMERS' REACTIONS

Mark Assini is Product Marketing Manager at Voices.com, and he vividly remembers one mistake he made early in his product marketing career around pricing. He said:

> I was working at an organization where pricing had been rightfully transferred from product to product marketing. After taking pricing under the product marketing umbrella, I conducted some analysis and realized that the price to value and discounting ratios were off. In other words, the organization was offering the best discounts and higher

volumes at its lowest price points and offering the worst discounts and lower volumes at its highest price points. This meant that customers had zero incentive to spend more at higher price points; in fact, they were losing value and spending more by doing so. Most customers expect to get more by spending more, not the opposite.

After realizing this, I developed a new pricing strategy that corrected the inconsistencies and reoriented the price to value and discount ratios. Thinking I had done a good job, and getting the approval from my manager, we rolled out the new pricing. Unsurprisingly, our customers were less than thrilled. They went from getting the best deals at the lowest price points, to having to spend more to get the same value. I had made the fatal mistake of not considering customer reactions and perception, instead prioritizing the business's revenue health. Needless to say, it was a tough couple of months for our customer support team, as they dealt with countless complaints. While we had messaging in place to address the concerns, the organization felt the pain of the change for longer than any had expected.

As the saying goes, time heals all, and eventually our customers, especially new ones, got used to the new pricing, and revenue eventually recovered and in fact, combined with some other product-related changes, increased. While the ending was a positive one, living it was at times less than enjoyable, for me and for our customers.

## LEARN TO LET GO

Patrick Cuttica is former Director of Product Marketing at Sprout Social. At the time, his team consisted of him and five other go-to-market strategists (product marketing managers), and they were in charge of the commercialization of their product strategy. This included tactical work like communicating and facilitating releases and updates of existing features and products, but it was also highly strategic work like establishing core product positioning and leveraging customer data and qualitative insights to support product decision-making.

Over the last six years, Patrick has also helped to launch new disciplines:

> I like to think about product marketing at Sprout sort of like an incubator. We were sort of the sales enablement team before a real sales enablement team was hired. We were also the beginnings of customer marketing and onboarding before we hired formal teams for that. So we've done a lot over the years, but the core has always been that we are the go-to-market strategists.

> A mistake that I've made in the past was not knowing when it's time to pass some of those things we've incubated on. Or not being willing to let them go. It can be hard to let go of programs or initiatives that you've helped to build. But ultimately, that's why you hire and how you grow.

As a leader I'm constantly having to reinvent myself, and my team has to, too, as we are constantly taking on new challenges. Otherwise, we risk being stuck doing reactive work—that's lower impact, when we could be more focused and strategic.

## UNDERSTAND LOCAL NEEDS

Collette Johnson, Product Marketing Strategist at Redgate Software, tells us:

I remember when I was working in consultancy, a product failed massively. They were launching in Japan and the product all went wrong. This happened because there was a national holiday in Japan for a new emperor and Japan was going on a national holiday, and they just hadn't figured it out. They should have looked at their global calendars, just a small thing, but it would have made a massive difference. If you've never had that issue or nobody's ever talked to you about that issue, you will never understand how important that is.

If you work in the Asia market, you need to account for Chinese New Year, and so many marketers don't. If there's a national election on, it's not the time to launch a new product. In Europe, don't bother launching anything in the holiday season (July or August); wait until September. It can have such an implication on your outcome. Marketing's about timeliness. It's about understanding the local market. It's about understanding those people and their local and cultural needs. Not everyone has the same breaks as we do in the UK/Europe.

# CHAPTER 11

# BECOME AN EXPERT

You shouldn't stop striving once you feel you've nailed your internal positioning and have gained the respect of those you work with. You should do all you can to keep learning and growing.

In this section of the book, we will:

- Guide you on how you can gain the expertise you need to be a world-class product marketer.
- Share best practices from leading PMMs.
- Encourage you to take the next steps in your career.

## WHY IT'S CRUCIAL

Product managers might be the ones that are ultimately building the products and have the greatest in-depth technical knowledge around the products, but you should strive to try to match them as much as possible as far as technical knowledge goes. You will just be less connected to the engineering department on exactly what is being built from a code level than they are from understanding why it's being built.

It's important in terms of your internal image credibility that you have a high level of expertise in the products you manage. You want to be seen as an internal go-to as well.

It can look bad if you're in a meeting and get asked a question about the product and have to say, "Sorry, let me just go ask product management." You need that knowledge to be able to confidently position products yourself and ask questions.

More often than not, as the product marketer, you'll be the person who is actually presenting the product externally too. You'll be getting technical questions from customers and potential customers, so you need to be on a level—certainly these days—with SaaS business.

Patrick Cuttica, former Director of Product Marketing at Sprout Social and now Senior Product Marketing Manager at Square, adds, "In our job descriptions, we explicitly state, 'You possess the desire and capacity to garner a deep product knowledge while understanding the need to zoom out and tell concrete, compelling, benefit-focused stories about our platform and solutions. Your skills are part creative, part analytical, and always centered around delivering relevant content that enhances our brand.' Being an expert on the product doesn't mean having all the answers, but it does mean knowing where to go to get the answer."

## HOW TO GO ABOUT GETTING THE EXPERTISE

You can become an expert whether you've worked for short periods of time at several companies or whether you've been at one company for a substantial amount of time. You may have worked in one industry or more; this shouldn't impact your ability to become a subject matter expert.

Organizations are growing and changing, and you can grow by moving to a different product or feature internally. You should continue to relearn and understand different ways of touching on different audiences.

Here are some simple—yet effective—methods on how to acquire subject matter expertise:

- Sit down with your product's product manager and get them to give you an uber in-depth demo of all the nooks and crannies, and ask lots of questions. If you're not sure how something works or why a certain feature functions the way it does, this is your opportunity to get answers.

- Book some time with the product's engineers. You will likely have gleaned much of this information via the

PM, but as they say, knowledge is power, and hearing two people talking through the same product(s) is a great way to ensure you're 100 percent grounded on the ins and outs of it. Having a one-on-one with engineering is never a bad thing when it comes to relationship-building either. And again, don't be afraid of asking lots of questions.

- Spend plenty of time actually using the product. Go through the motions and processes your various personas would go through, and stress test every inch of it. If you're new to a product, you'll want to spend several hours doing this over your first few weeks. Once you're more settled in, we'd still recommend spending an hour or so a month doing this to ensure your knowledge around this area remains tip-top, and that you're familiar with any updates—no matter how big or small.

- If possible, dedicate some time to watching customers use the product. This will add another layer to your knowledge of how it works and how your audience uses it. You might also want to shadow a few product demos (if applicable) to get a feel for the types of questions customers and prospects put forward.

- Block out time to immerse yourself in all the marketing, sales, and customer-facings assets at your company's disposal—this could be anything from product manuals and sales one-pagers to whitepapers or webinars.

- Research, research, and research some more. As well as your own product(s), this extends to your competitors' products, your customers, your industry, adjacent markets, and so on. Your data points are water; you're the sponge. Absorb as much as you can and then filter that information through to the relevant people/teams.

When it comes to becoming an SME on product marketing itself, it's essential you devote ample time to studying and upskilling—commit to this by blocking some time out in your calendar either weekly or monthly. If you have a product marketing team, internal "lunch 'n' learn" type sessions are a great way to knowledge-share and bring everyone up to the same level. However, even if you do have a team to lean on, we'd still recommend seeking external resources. This way, you don't run the risk of becoming too warped by your own internal best practices and processes and missing out on emerging trends, topics, and tactics other specialists are playing elsewhere.

Solely learning on the job in your company will only get you so far. You want to learn actual methodologies on what you do.

We've infused the experiences of others into every single page of this book, but there's so much more out there too. Without wanting to plug our own stuff too much, if you haven't already, do check out our Slack channel—thousands of PMMs all over the world are in there, every day, sharing their advice, experiences, and solutions. It's a constant hive of help and inspiration.

There are other ways too:

- Connect with people you want to learn from on LinkedIn. No harm ever came from asking someone if they have time for a chat. If they say no, you've not lost anything. If they say yes, you can tap into their expertise.

- Tune in to podcast or video shows. These usually feature very well-known, experienced guests that you can learn a lot from, for free.

- Attend an event. Again, these usually feature some of the best PMMs around and are a great way to not only learn from them but network with lots more of your product marketing peers.

- If you're after something more long term and formal, find yourself a product marketing mentor or coach.

- Take a product marketing course and align yourself to industry gold standards. Courses can help you understand the methodologies, the principles, and the practices you need so you can shape your role as a product marketer.

## THE DIFFERENCE NAILING YOUR
## INTERNAL POSITIONING CAN MAKE

How you position your product has a knock-on effect on every-thing you do as a product marketer. You can have an eye-catching social media ad, the most creative email campaign, and the best-written landing page on the planet, but if your positioning is off, the product still won't sell.

In many ways, the same applies to your internal positioning. If you don't frame yourself, your role, and your function in the right way, you make a rod for your own back. Even with the most compelling customer research, people may not take notice. You can have the greatest go-to-market strategy, but others won't pull their weight. You can have the most innovative ideas, but people won't hear them.

When you nail your internal positioning, it gives you more cred-ibility, more bandwidth, and more buy-in. You'll get more sup-port and cooperation from other teams, which will ultimately make your life easier. You'll be appreciated and taken seriously. You won't have to keep explaining what you do; people will auto-matically trust you, and this will give you more scope to carry out your job.

If you want to reach your potential, you need to lay this ground-work because once people understand and appreciate what you do, the rest will take care of itself. You'll have a voice, and it will be heard, and people will buy into what you say and do. This, as any product marketer will tell you, is mission critical to your success.

Throughout this book, we've taken you on a tour of some of the most common tactics those in the industry employ, and if you make a concerted effort to apply at least *some* (ideally all!) of these ideas, we are certain you'll see a tangible difference. And remember, real change can take time.